The Stress-Proof Child

The Stress-Proof Child

A Loving Parent's Guide

ANTOINETTE SAUNDERS, PH.D.,
and BONNIE REMSBERG

HOLT, RINEHART and WINSTON New York

First published in January 1985 by Holt, Rinehart and Winston,
383 Madison Avenue, New York, New York 10017.
Published simultaneously in Canada by Holt, Rinehart and
Winston of Canada, Limited.

Library of Congress Cataloging in Publication Data
Saunders, Antoinette.
The stress-proof child.
Bibliography: p. 215
Includes index.
1. Problem children.   2. Stress in children.
3. Parenting.   I. Remsberg, Bonnie.   II. Title.
HQ773.S22   1984   649'.153   84-9041
ISBN 0-03-069656-9

First Edition

Design by Ellen Lo Giudice
Printed in the United States of America
3   5   7   9   10   8   6   4   2

ISBN 0-03-069656-9

For Boni and Jenny and Rich

ACKNOWLEDGMENTS

We are grateful to Annie Moldafsky, who brought us together; Peter and Barbara Dyson, who helped us start; Betsy Joyce, who typed our manuscript; Jennifer Josephy, our editor; Gail Cutler, who helped with the chapter on nutrition; Laurel Houser-Flemming, who contributed to the bibliography; and all of the children.

Sick

"I cannot go to school today,"
Said little Peggy Ann McKay.
"I have the measles and the mumps,
A gash, a rash and purple bumps.
My mouth is wet, my throat is dry,
I'm going blind in my right eye.
My tonsils are as big as rocks,
I've counted sixteen chicken pox.
And there's one more—that's seventeen,
And don't you think my face looks green?
My leg is cut, my eyes are blue—
It might be instamatic flu.
I cough and sneeze and gasp and choke,
I'm sure that my left leg is broke—
My hip hurts when I move my chin,
My belly button's caving in,
My back is wrenched, my ankle's sprained,
My 'pendix pains each time it rains.
My nose is cold, my toes are numb,
I have a sliver in my thumb.
My neck is stiff, my spine is weak,
I hardly whisper when I speak.
My tongue is filling up my mouth,
I think my hair is falling out.
My elbow's bent, my spine ain't straight,
My temperature is one-o-eight.
My brain is shrunk, I cannot hear.
There is a hole inside my ear.
I have a hangnail, and my heart is—What?
What's that? What's that you say?
You say today is . . . Saturday?
G'bye. I'm going out to play!"

—*Shel Silverstein*

CONTENTS

INTRODUCTION

My hope in writing this book is to give children and their parents help in identifying and conquering stress. Ever since I began stress-education classes for children, many people have said to me, "But kids don't have stress."

Those people must not know any kids.

I never have to explain to kids what I mean when talking about stress. They don't need to be convinced. They may need to be told about how stress actually affects their bodies, how it causes their headaches and their stomachaches, but once they make that connection, they understand there is something they can do to feel better. They know they have stress; what they need is to learn how to handle it. As the world gets noisier, more complicated, and more exciting, we face the challenge of preparing our children for it. They can learn to thrive on it rather than die from it.

The first step in dealing with this complicated world is to make a commitment: "I will take responsibility for my own life." Once you have made your commitment, then you can teach your children to do the same.

To begin, I want to tell you a little about myself and my reason for writing this book.

I lost both of my parents when I was seven years old. My father died; soon after, my mother was hospitalized for emotional problems, then died. I was sent away to boarding schools and summer camps. For many years I was separated from my brothers and sisters, aunts and uncles. With no family around to help me grow, I had to find my way on my own.

I could have become depressed and withdrawn, even psychotic, but I knew instinctively that I wanted to survive. I decided not to waste energy feeling sorry for myself. Instead, I put whatever energy I could muster into developing a winning personality, being endearing. It worked so well that several of my friends' parents volunteered to adopt me. What had happened to me, of course, is that I found, in popularity, a way to get the approval and attention that I so badly needed.

Since becoming a psychologist, I have researched deeply into children's abilities to adapt. I realize that that is what I did as a child: I adapted. I also realize how resourceful and strong I was. I marvel at how resourceful and strong most children are.

I started out intending to become a nurse, attempting to heal the wounds of others the way I wanted my own wounds healed. But it wasn't satisfying, because it wasn't direct enough. So I went into psychology.

After graduate school, I taught for six years in the pediatrics and child-psychiatry departments of a medical school. There I worked with families who were in the deepest stress imaginable: their children were dying.

For me, each day carried tremendous pain. In each child, I relived my own parents' deaths. I found this work very taxing. I was beginning to doubt my ability to cope and to be helpful to my patients and their families. One day it occurred to me that I was being unnecessarily hard on myself—that the demands of the work I was doing were incredibly difficult in their own right and that, in addition, I was bringing in all the unresolved pain of my own childhood. I decided I was doing the best I could and that as I had more experience I would do even better. And it worked! I was able to help the children and their families despite the pain I felt.

Once past my own personal barrier, I started looking closely at the children. All of them, no matter how sick they were emotionally or physically, responded to the same techniques. I could teach them to relax, to believe in themselves, to know and respect their bodies, to solve problems, and to articulate their needs.

Most important, I taught them how to convey this information to their parents. Unfortunately, many children don't feel that this option is open to them. Because they don't know any better, many children set themselves up so that nobody listens to them. Their behavior may be destructive, worrisome, or just obnoxious.

Adults often don't stop to think, "This is a troubled child." Their response to such children, instead, is that they wish them out of the way, off the scene. That's how we end up with so many "throwaway" children.

When I began a clinical practice with an emphasis on the problems of children, I started noticing that parents were bringing children to me who were suffering—and I do mean suffering—from headaches, stomachaches, even ulcers and hypertension, that had no organic cause.

At the time, the subject of stress-related diseases among adults was beginning to receive considerable public attention. The code words then were "executive stress." But as far as I could discern, no one was connecting stress with its effect on the health and well-being of children.

Seemingly unrelated factors began to connect in my mind. The evidence I was hearing about the effects of stress on the body made complete sense to me. The work I had done with chronically ill children had already shown me, often in graphic ways, that attitudes affect health. I became increasingly sensitive to and respectful of the connection between mind and body. Intrigued by this, I traveled to Texas to study with Carl and Stephanie Simonton, about whom you will read more in this book. The Simontons work with cancer patients and believe that people's attitudes and life-styles contribute to their getting sick and can affect their getting well. Watching them practice, I saw the validity of this premise demonstrated again and again.

I began to think about these insights as they relate to children. Why, I wondered, if we can figure out the reason people get sick from their stress and we can teach them how to get well again, can we not teach children how to prevent themselves from getting sick in the first place? At that time, I was consulting at two elementary schools in Skokie, Illinois, near where I live and practice. I asked permission to set up stress-management classes for children there. I was given an eighth-grade class and a mixed class of fourth-, fifth-, and sixth-graders.

The classes were an instant success! The children loved the curriculum and told me that they found it helpful and meaningful. Because of their reactions, I realized that I had opened up an area of education that could be very important to all children. I decided to take seriously this new area that I was exploring, so I set up stress-education clinics for children in my office as part of my practice. That was several years ago, and by now those sessions too have proved to be a big success. Enrollment is full; the parents and children have been delighted with the results. The clinics run for ten weeks. At the first session, I meet with the parents, then at eight weekly sessions, I teach children from six to fourteen how to recognize and handle stress in their lives. At the final session, parents and children meet together.

It is too soon to determine the long-term results required by a truly scientific experiment; for that we would have to wait for all the children who have been through my clinics thus far to grow up and report back on their health conditions. But I can tell you that the comments I hear from the children have convinced me that stress education has made a major difference in their lives.

They tell me that they feel better about themselves,

that they like themselves better. And they feel, after stress education, that they have tools and attitudes with which they can handle the stress that they inevitably encounter. Their parents report being impressed with changes for the better in their children.

It has been an exciting adventure. Both parents and children have expressed gratitude for the opportunity to learn these tools and techniques. It seemed only logical, as the next step, to put my stress-education curriculum into a book, so that these tools and techniques can be made available to parents and children everywhere.

Now that you know something about me and my background, I would like you to know a bit about my coauthor, Bonnie Remsberg. Whenever I think about this book—how it came about and what I hope for it to accomplish—I realize that while I provided its body, it was Bonnie who breathed life into it. She is a professional journalist with more than twenty years experience in writing for parents and children. She has had articles in all the major women's magazines and has award-winning television documentaries to her credit; she also has taught writing courses at major universities. But just as important, she and I think alike. While we have chosen to use the first-person form throughout this book, the attitudes and values expressed here are hers as well as mine. Indeed, guided by them, she has raised a daughter and son to productive adulthood. She has been, in many ways that are validating for us both, a laboratory for the techniques of stress management presented here.

These techniques have been thoroughly tested on real children like yours. When each child completes my series of classes, I give him or her a button that reads THE CAPABLE KID. The children have been delighted and proudly wear their buttons and confident smiles.

Isn't that what all parents want their children to be—

capable kids, emotionally equipped to face whatever life hands to them? With the program outlined in this book, children will be able to recognize the headaches, stomachaches, neck aches, and worse that come from stress. Their tantrums will go away and their bed-wetting will stop.

Best of all, they will be able to look forward to an adulthood in which they have the tools to manage stress. If you are the person who gives them these tools, you will give them an inheritance more precious than gold. You will give them the means to be happy.

PART 1

Recognizing Children's Stress

1

What It's All About

"When we get nervous or upset our bodies react to our feelings by doing various things. Sometimes people get headaches when they feel upset. Other people might get knots or butterflies in their stomach. Sometimes you get a lump in your throat. Or wobbly knees. Those body signs or body cues are telling you that you are nervous or upset."

—Lisa Hild, age 10½

What We Want Our Children to Be—Capable Kids

You know the kind of child you want to raise. You know that child when you meet him. He may be black, white, tall, short, thick, thin, musical, athletic or not. But he *is* a capable child. He meets his challenges. He is calm and confident. He is coping. *

What does a child who is coping look like? In my experience, he stands straight, looks you in the eye, and talks

*Throughout this book the pronouns *he*, *him*, and *his* will be used in the singular when referring to all children, male and female.

confidently and honestly about what he is doing. A calm, confident child shows genuine interest in what other people are doing. Children who are coping well are energetic and spontaneous, soft, sensitive, responsive to other people. They enjoy humor. They are responsible. When a crisis occurs, they are reflective and helpful. There is a peacefulness about these children. When you are with them, *you* feel calm and proud.

Evaluating Your Child's Vulnerability to Stress

Who is that child you love? How does he think? What does he feel? As a parent, *you* will feel more confident, more capable, if you can understand what is going on inside your child. If you can see inside him, you can help him grow up happy and well.

I will say it often; it cannot be said often enough: the children who deal best with stress are those who have self-confidence. Their behavior makes clear whether or not they do. The ways in which they act show us, every day, how they feel about themselves. All we need to do is learn to read their clues. A parent can learn to read a child the way he or she would read a road map. Observing your child's behavior can "de-code" him for you.

A Capable Kid Is

spontaneous
active, energetic
happy
capable of getting excited about good things
resourceful*
confident*
opinionated but open to new ideas

reflective
thoughtful, sensitive to others
physically affectionate
able to confront people when concerned or upset
    about something*
willing to take risks
fond of himself
relaxed*
responsible*
helpful
cooperative
able to express feelings easily*
able to feel things intensely

A Capable Kid Also

has a sense of direction*
has goals and ambitions
has a sense of humor
has good eye contact
can postpone gratification
seeks help when he needs it
owns up to his mistakes

A Vulnerable Kid Is

overly sensitive, shy
moody, irritable
withdrawn, preoccupied†
hesitant
frequently sick without organic cause†
constantly in need of reassurance
defenseless
given to overuse of the phrase *I don't know*

---

* These are the most important characteristics of the Capable Kid.
†Indicates *very* serious signs of vulnerability.

lonely and not able to make friends
dependent, clinging
frequently frightened
isolated†
secretive, noncommunicative†
defensive
resistant to being touched or hugged
clumsy, accident prone
belligerent, uncooperative†
easily angered
constantly complaining
stubborn
subject to frequent unexplained aches and pains
unable to concentrate
impatient
unable to regulate eating, taking in either too much
    or too little
generally negative in attitude
impulsive
often tired
a poor performer in school and capable of doing
    better
overactive, frenetic

A Vulnerable Kid Also

has problems going to sleep
has poor eye contact
has a nervous laugh
has nervous tics
stutters
grinds his teeth
has frequent severe nightmares†
bites his nails
wets his bed

†Indicates *very* serious signs of vulnerability.

lies or distorts†
takes things that don't belong to him

Go over both lists. Place a check mark next to any behavior that is characteristic of your child. Soon, a pattern will begin to emerge. If most of your check marks are on the Capable Kid list, then that is the kind of child you are raising. Let me congratulate you. You have been doing a good job with your child. You have told him how much you love and respect him, not only through your words, but in your actions. You will enjoy reading this book for reassurance, to see how well you have been doing!

In the Vulnerable Kid list a score of one to seven indicates that your child is slightly vulnerable. Seven to fifteen is moderately vulnerable. Fifteen and above is very vulnerable and very serious.

If your check marks form a pattern that shows a Vulnerable Kid, you have work to do. The fact that you are reading this book proves that you are concerned enough to want to help your child, and, therefore, you can.

I hope that your child falls into the Capable Kid category. If he does not, he may simply be overwhelmed. And what is overwhelming him is stress.

What Is Stress?

Stress is any extra demand made on the body. Our twentieth-century bodies react to danger in exactly the same way primitive man's body reacted: a hormonal surge that enables us to flee or to fight.

Depending on the perceived danger or stress, our autonomic nervous system releases hormones causing chemical changes. Our hearts beat faster, our breathing speeds up, and blood flows into our brains.

Because we have the same physical reaction regardless of whether the stress is negative or positive, Hans Selye, the pioneer of stress research, called this response the General Adaptation Syndrome.

In our modern, complicated world, which places extra demands on us all, this primitive response to flee or fight is no longer efficient. Yet like primitive man, we tend to *react* to these demands rather than to reflect and evaluate them.

When we don't deal with the chronic stress in our lives, our bodies suffer never-ending wear and tear from the flight-or-fight response. If we don't learn to deal well with our stresses, we can develop headaches, backaches, ulcers, heart attacks, and a long list of annoying, damaging, and sometimes very serious ailments.

Our children live in the same stressful, complicated world. Their bodies have the same biochemical reaction to stress. They develop headaches, backaches, stomachaches, and other ills in the same way adults do.

Our children experience the stress of illness, divorce, financial problems, living with single parents, death, school, remarriage, jealousy, achievement, vacations, stepbrothers and -sisters, sex, drugs, sensory bombardment, violence, the threat of nuclear war—a long, long list.

The effect can be overwhelming.

What Children Need—Validation and Security

How can we help our children deal with stress? How can we create an atmosphere in which our children feel validated and secure? What do these terms mean, and why are they important? A child who is validated feels, "I am okay. I like myself. I am a valuable person." A child who is secure feels confident that no matter what happens to him or around him he will survive it.

As the world becomes more and more complicated, especially for children, this tendency to become overwhelmed gets more and more common. Stress in and of itself is not a bad thing. Stress can and does push us into accomplishment all the time. Each of us has numerous positive examples in our lives of where such a push has led us.

What does cause problems, for our children as well as for us, is a lack of ability to deal with stress. Children who feel emotionally isolated, who feel they lack the support to face the challenges of their lives, are the children who do not handle stress well. Children need tools for dealing with stress. Troubled children are not troubled by stress itself; they are troubled by their own feelings of isolation. They see stress as problems, rather than opportunities. Faced with enough problems, they can become inundated with their feelings of isolation and can become truly problem children. And that is what you, the parent, can prevent.

A safe and confirming atmosphere is essential to give children the sense that they can cope. We must give our children the skills and supports to deal with whatever happens to them. Furthermore, we must convince them that they have those skills. They must be able to feel confident, to walk straight and tall, to look life in the eye. If they feel that they have the internal resources to do this, if they know when and how to reach out for help, then there isn't anything they can't do. If you can give your children those skills and that confidence, you have given them the greatest gift of all.

We also *validate* our children by giving them the feeling that, at any given moment, they are doing all right, and that even though they are less than perfect, they are still acceptable, lovable people. This means we must convey the feeling that we know that, at this time, they are

doing their best. That doesn't mean that they can't do better. Often, of course, they can and must learn to do better. But when children misbehave you can learn to use
that occasion as an opportunity to correct their behavior
in a way that helps them grow but doesn't undermine
their self-confidence.

Touching is another way that we validate children. I
cannot emphasize enough the importance of touching
your children. Physical contact is vitally important to all of
us. Unfortunately, in our society we have sexualized
touching and, therefore, we prohibit it in situations where
it could and would do us good. We have made up rules
that inhibit us from touching each other. But for children,
as it should be for adults, touching is a way of saying, "I
really like you. I really like touching you. Your body feels
good to me." That is how infants learn to feel good about
themselves. They experience joy and satisfaction from the
touching and stroking their parents give them. If they get
the message that they feel good to touch, then they learn
to feel good about themselves.

Another vital part of validating our children is *listening*
to them. More than anything, it lets them know how important they are and that what they have to say is important. It lets them know they are important to *us*.

Children are enormously sensitive about not being listened to or taken seriously. In my practice, I spend a
great deal of time teaching children how to talk in a way
that is easier for adults to listen to. Unfortunately, many
children chatter and babble. They talk in ways that annoy
and irritate adults. They may be loud or silly. They may
whine. Often they don't seem to make sense. Given the
opportunity and loving encouragement, children can
learn to shorten their stories, make their points clearer, or
say things in a way that makes sense to adults. Children
are grateful when given nonjudgmental, noncritical
coaching, because they really are anxious to be listened to
and validated.

After validation, the second step in creating a confident, calm child is building an atmosphere of *security*. Parents have been told over and over about the importance of consistency. In my practice as a child psychologist, the issue of consistency comes up all the time. Children are constantly looking for limits. They look for *consistency* because it means that whomever they depend on is putting energy and effort and love into caring for them. Children experience this as attention being paid to them. When you are consistent, you are saying to them that taking care of them is important to you, that they are important to you. A child experiences this care and attention as love.

The two other necessary components to security are *honesty* and *openness*. Many parents feel that they need to protect their children from what is really going on in the world or in their marital relationship or in their finances. My experience has shown that no matter how thorough the attempt to cover up, children know just what is going on in a family's life. They may not be able to discuss it as you or I might. They don't have the sophistication to put it into words, and they may not even want to. Still, they know when something is amiss.

When their parents try to protect them from the truth, the discrepancy between what they experience going on and what they are told is going on frightens them. This kind of dishonesty makes children suspicious about the adults who take care of them.

Children need to know that adults are in charge. This does not necessarily mean that adults have all the answers to all the questions. But if children feel that we are being honest with them, that we are doing the best we can, and that we are trying to make the best choices, that is all they need to know. This knowledge calms them down and makes them feel good about themselves and their environment. When they know that the adults responsible for them are in charge and are doing a good job, they can

relax. Seeing this relaxation, this trust, in a child is a
beautiful sight.

The other ingredient of honesty is openness. I think it
is very important that parents be open with their children. There are few things that children should be kept
from knowing. But one of those few, I think, because it
involves maturity and privacy, is their parents' sexual and
intimate relationship.

Children are not responsible for solving problems, but
they certainly have a right to know what is going on in
their family. Children need information, for example, on
financial issues within the family. They should share in
the family's problems, but not feel that they alone have
the burden of solving them. They must feel that they are a
part of the family, a unit that values their involvement.

Once you have set the tone for your children by validating them and making them feel secure, then they have
the tools and the reassurance that they can deal with anything that comes along.

We are all formed, in our early years, by people's expectations of us. We grow up mirroring the images of
others. Children, including yours, are self-fulfilling
prophecies. They become to a large extent what people
say and think about them. Tell a child often enough that
he is a bad boy, that he is naughty and lazy, and sure
enough, he will become an adult who feels himself to be
unworthy. Tell a little girl that she is pretty but dumb,
and she will grow up feeling confident about her looks and
inadequate to take on the world. Selma Fraiberg, in her
admirable book on early child development, *The Magic
Years*, states, ". . . the child who is made to feel worthless
and degraded for his childhood offenses will come to believe in his own worthlessness and unlovability and out of
this degradation of the self come the mental cripples and
outcasts of our society."

A Little Boy Called "Power"

Paul K. is an amazingly bright ten-year-old. He is small for his age and could pass for eight or nine. His mother, a bright, thoughtful woman, is also small and delicate looking. Paul's father, a corporate lawyer, spends most of his waking hours working or thinking about work. The family is rather isolated. Paul is their only child. Mrs. K. had a difficult pregnancy and Paul was born with a heart murmur. Mrs. K. tends to overprotect him.

To Paul, the world is frustrating. His parents, who value dignity and respect for elders, are baffled by Paul's angry outbursts. As he tries to adapt to a public elementary school where the children are verbally and physically aggressive, he finds he can't compete physically because he is small and his parents don't allow him to "talk back" or be "disrespectful." Paul feels trapped, living in two different worlds and belonging to neither.

So Paul has created a third world. It is a world of Greek mythology, where he is powerful. He calls himself "Power." He identifies with Zeus. Paul has read everything he can get his hands on about Greek mythology. He knows more than most children do on the subject. Few adults could challenge him on the depth of his knowledge.

The world Paul has created on Mount Olympus is a safe place for him to live. There he battles with other gods and always wins. When he talks of the friendships he has there, they are always successful. He is accepted and liked.

This fantasy world is Paul's creative way of dealing with his frustration at being powerless and of feeling isolated. The many characters he has to research and organize keep him busy and make him feel important.

But Paul, who probably has close to a genius IQ, is not finishing his schoolwork and, as a result, is getting into trouble. Like all children, he is hungry for attention, so he finds ways to get people involved with him. One of the techniques that gets him attention is not handing in his homework. Although he is being threatened with the possibility of not passing, he can't seem to focus. He gets distracted by his thoughts about Mount Olympus or by what other children are doing. He yearns to get along with others and be a part of a group.

There is no question that Paul's parents love him very much. Yet things they do out of their love for him, based on their own upbringing, he experiences as rejection. "Don't be angry," his mom says. "It hurts me when you talk to me that way." His dad says, "Not now, I'm too tired." Paul experiences these as rejections, which make him furious. Then he goes to school where, because of his size and his "different" ways, the children treat him like an outsider. Wherever he is, he feels out of place.

Like all children, Paul needs to know that he is important and to feel that he is accepted. His parents need to validate Paul, to make him feel important in positive ways. For example, by

> not overprotecting him. (Children experience over-protection as a statement of their inability to handle things.)
>
> giving him opportunities to do things on his own: going to the store, visiting friends, having responsibility around the house other than the garbage, e.g., planning meals or family activities.
>
> giving him opportunities in school to lead projects, help other children. This is necessary so that he receives the attention he desires.
>
> having the family (especially the father and son) say the Good-night Formula to each other. (See the exercise at the end of this chapter. Paul needs validating, and the formula is a good technique for validating children.)

THE CAPABLE-KID STRESS TEST

How well does your child handle stress? This test was developed to give you a quick, simple way of determining how your child handles a stressful situation.

1. Think of a situation that your child has experienced as stressful. It might be sharing a room with his brother, canceling plans for a weekend, flunking a test, not making the team, being teased, getting embarrassed, and so on

2. Think about how he reacted to that situation.

3. Now choose *one* statement that best describes how he would react. (Choose the one that stands out immediately.)

    a. "Things like this always happen to me."†

    b. Becomes unreasonably quiet and walks away.†

    c. "I never get what I want; you guys don't care about me." (Becomes belligerent and verbally abusive.)*

    d. "I am disappointed. [Then seconds later:] Oh well, maybe next time."

    e. "This is not a surprise. I was expecting this." (Then becomes withdrawn and preoccupied.)*

    f. "That makes me angry, but I didn't know. Is there anything I can do to help?"

    g. "That's not fair." (Screams and yells.)†

    h. Doesn't visibly react, just withdraws; doesn't talk about it, isolates himself.*

4. Find the description of your child.

d or f   *Capable Kid.* He handles stress well. The Capable Kid will express his disappointment or anger and then quickly figure out what to do

---

*Continues to respond this way for over twenty-four hours.

†Doesn't take him very long (a couple of hours at the most) to bounce back and start to think about what he can do to make things better.

about it. He will be disappointed rather than upset. This disappointment will last only min utes.

a, b, or g   *Slightly Vulnerable Kid.* This slightly vulnerable child has upset reactions, but they are short-lived. The child calms down, becomes less preoccupied with himself, and begins to make such statements as "Oh well. I can rearrange my schedule."

While this child doesn't need professional help, he could benefit from learning more effective coping strategies so as to become less reactive. See chapters 6, 8, 10, and 11 for techniques to help this child.

c, e, h   *Seriously Vulnerable Kid.* This child may need professional help. His response lasts longer than twenty-four hours. He displays symptoms of the Vulnerable Kid list (see pages 11–12).

The Effects of Stress

In my stress-education classes I teach children what stress is and how it works on their bodies. I teach them how the mind and the body work, how our bodies don't lie to us and are constantly giving us messages, letting us know how we *really* feel about things. We talk, for example, about someone who is a "pain in the neck." We have "splitting" headaches when, for some reason, we feel torn. All we have to do is learn to listen to our body's reactions so we can find out how a situation is affecting us.

Here is how one of the older children explained stress in class:

Stress affects our bodies. For example, when you are upset about a test you might get a stomachache, or you might not feel hungry when you would normally be starved. Some people when they are "nervous" or under stress, might talk fast or bite their nails.

Each person responds to stress differently. It's important for you to know how your body responds to stress. Sometimes we are upset about something and we don't even know it until our body "tells" us by giving us a headache, a neckache, sweaty palms, or palpitations.

Think about the last time you were under stress. What happened to your body? Did you get

sweaty palms?
upset stomach?
headache?
heart pounding?
forgetful?
bitten nails?
fast breathing?
dry mouth?
weak knees?
unexplained fever?
angry?
shaky hands?
tightening muscles?
upsetting thoughts?
loss of confidence?
stuttering?
twitching muscles?
neckache?
afraid of something bad happening?
loss of appetite?
sleeplessness?
nauseated?

In the stress clinic, I teach children how to relax, because the core element of stress management is being re flective rather than reactive. For primitive man, fight or flee was an impulsive, spontaneous reaction to what was happening. Modern man's reaction to stress has to be less instinctive and more thoughtful. When something is happening to us, instead of reacting automatically, we need to slow down in order to slow down the physiological response that makes our hearts pound faster and our breathing increase. It is important to think about what is happening so that we can make more constructive and valuable choices.

Getting angry and acting out their feelings, or "popping off," is a common reaction to stress for children. This is the "fight" in the flight-fight response. Many children equate stress with anger, because stressful situations often make them angry.

Here is a ten-year-old boy's drawing about how stress works. He came to these conclusions after studying stress in my classes.

He received a report card with very bad marks. He became angry at himself and turned his anger inward, developing a bellyache, and outward, by swearing. Then he decided, "Well, if I try harder, I can do better." So he calmed himself down. Then he felt stronger and stronger.

Illness—the Mind-Body Connection

You have heard people say, "If you keep your feelings bottled up inside, you will get sick." They are right.

The literature on psychosomatic medicine describes in detail the interaction between the mind and the body. "There is a clear link between stress and illness, a link so strong that it is possible to predict illness based on the amount of stress in peoples' lives," report Carl and

Report Card

	Grade
Grammar	F-
Math	F
Soc. Studies	F+
Science	D+

Arrgh!!
I got 3 F's and
1 D+.!!
I HATE
Myself!

Bellyache

Stress
(swearing)

Well, I did get
a D+. If I tried
harder I could do
better.

Calming Down

Growing Stronger

Supra-Strong

Made by: Powell.T.K

Stephanie Simonton in their excellent book *Getting Well Again*. Much of the early work demonstrating that emotional conditions can have an effect on illness was undertaken by Hans Selye at the University of Prague in the 1920s.

For years, physicians have observed that illness is more likely to occur following highly stressful events in people's lives. Many doctors have noticed that when their patients suffered major emotional upsets there was an increase in not only diseases usually acknowledged to be susceptible to emotional influence—ulcers, high blood pressure, heart disease, headaches—but also in infectious diseases, backaches, and even accidents.

Why We Need Stress

Hans Selye states that stress is the spice of life. It stimulates us to be creative, to progress, to solve problems, to change. Without stress, we complain of boredom, fatigue. We are frustrated and dissatisfied.

With too much stress, however, we tend to be irritable. We don't problem-solve so effectively. We feel exhausted and may even get sick.

With too little stress, we are

bored
tired
frustrated
unhappy
prone to illness

With too much stress we are

irritable
overwhelmed

exhausted
unable to think clearly
prone to illness

With just the right amount we are

happy
motivated
productive

The good news about stress, which you can share with your child, is that we can change our experience of it so that it works for us. We can thrive on it and grow from it. We can view it as an opportunity.

We can change our experience of any situation just by changing our perception of it. For example, when I want to get someplace in my car and I'm running short of time, I feel as though I am "under a lot of stress." If I say to myself, "I'm going to get there when I'm going to get there, and this is really an opportunity for me to relax and listen to music on the radio," then the experience of being hassled changes into an opportunity to relax. Conquering stress is a matter of, as the old saying goes, taking a lemon and making lemonade.

Our minds are powerful, far more powerful than most of us realize. This is true not only of my mind and your mind, but of your child's mind as well. His mind, like yours or mine, is the most powerful organ in his body.

Your mind caused you to pick up this book. Your mind is telling you that you are a good parent and that you want to be a better one. Your mind, even now, is working on helping your child change his perception of stress.

You can help your child. Don't let yourself become discouraged. And don't think that you can accomplish all of your goals in a week. I have seen over and over that children find comfort just in the knowledge that their parents are trying to make things better.

No one expects you to be perfect. Certainly not your child. He knows that he is not perfect, so he fully expects you, like him, to be human and to make mistakes.

There is no such thing, anyway, as the perfect person or the perfect parent.

The most that any of us can do is try.

Exercise

THE GOOD-NIGHT FORMULA

Here is an exercise I use with parents who are concerned about their children's poor self-esteem. These are the children who do not feel good about themselves, who look and act depressed, who aren't excited about anything, who are self-critical and negative.

Set the Scene: I have found in my work with children how important the ritual around going to bed is for them. It seems that if parents are willing to devote fifteen minutes to their child at bedtime, that time counts for a lot. This fact always reassures busy career or single parents, and it should.

Create the Atmosphere: It's very important that the parent establish a warm, loving, accepting atmosphere for this exercise. Good eye contact and the chance for physical closeness is essential.

The Formula: The formula consists of four statements shared between the parent and child as part of saying good-night.

The parent and child *each* say the following, and after each statement is made, the partner repeats it until he has understood it correctly. (The first few times you may feel self-conscious doing this, but often people do misunderstand one another or just don't hear one another correctly.)

1. Something he likes about himself.
2. Something he did that day that he feels good about.
3. Something he is looking forward to doing tomorrow.
4. After each person has shared his or her statements, then an exchange of "I love you" is given, accompanied by a reassuring physical contact (a hug, squeezed hand, loving rub on the back).

An Opportunity for Modeling: This is a great opportunity for a parent to introduce to a child certain values about caring for himself and others.

For example, the parent makes these statements to his child:

1. A good feeling about the other: "I enjoyed having you help me with dinner." ; or "I like the way you told those jokes tonight."
2. Something he felt good about doing today: "I feel good about telling your mommy that I love her very much"; or "I listened to my secretary tell me how upset she is about work."
3. Something he is looking forward to tomorrow: "I am looking forward to talking to your teacher to-

morrow"; or "I am looking forward to watching you play basketball tomorrow."

Road Blocks: Be prepared. Not all children are going to respond easily to this exercise. The children who lack self-confidence or who are resistant because they are troubled will not cooperate at first, so it is very important to "hang in" with them. If your child is having a hard time coming up with statements, tell him the good things you feel about him, such as "I really like what you are wearing today; I know you put a lot of thought into putting your outfit together"; or "I really like the way you help your brother out." Or tell him something you like that he did that day: "I really appreciated how you helped me out with dinner tonight"; or "I really liked the fact that you fed the cat without my reminding you." Or relate something you hope he will look forward to doing tomorrow: "I just know you must be looking forward to spending the night with Jeanie tomorrow"; or "I know you must be looking forward to making those cookies with me tomorrow. I know I am."

Don't Give Up: Don't give up if it does not work at first. Your child might be testing you to see how much you believe in this exercise and how much you really care about him.

2

Looking Inside Your Child

You can learn to "read" the language of your child's feelings exactly the way you learned the language that enables you to read this book. Then you can do something about those feelings.

You, the parent, are the "doctor" for your child's feelings. As any good diagnostician knows, there is no use treating merely the symptoms. You have to get to the cause of the problem.

"It doesn't matter why she steals," a father once said to me about his daughter. "She steals, and stealing is bad."

But it does matter, very much. The little girl was not born a criminal. No one taught her to steal as a hobby or an occupation. She was doing it for a reason, and to her that reason appeared logical. Not right, of course, by her family's standards, or society's, or even by hers, but *logical*.

Have you ever seen a child throw a tantrum? Have you ever watched your *own* child throw a tantrum? Did it upset you? Anger you? Embarrass you? Maybe all three. Now, forget those feelings. Forget yourself. Concentrate for a moment on *why* the child threw the tantrum. What

31

was going on at that time in that child's head?

I remember throwing a tantrum once. I can recall it with crystal clarity. My feelings were so vivid to me that it might have happened yesterday. Yet the adults around me could not read those feelings.

I was about ten, lying on my bed in the dormitory in the convent boarding school. It was the middle of the day, and the dorm was empty except for a nun who was in the cubicle next to me. I could hear her moving around. At some level, I must have felt that that nun might be interested in me, but I wasn't sure.

I remember thrashing my legs and arms around on the bed and yelling out, "I want my mommy. I want my mommy." That was the first time I had said those words since I had lost my mother years before. It was as though something had welled up inside me, for whatever reason, and just burst out.

There is a pressure inside a child's tantrum, a need for recognition, and a need to go public with those intense feelings.

I was hoping that nun would respond to my pain. I was hoping to be held and comforted.

When children throw a tantrum, they are expressing their intense frustration and their inability to get the recognition and the reassurance that they need. In older children particularly, the ten- and eleven-year-olds, the tantrum represents a reaction to stress. They are frightened about something, and that something isn't being attended to. Their reaction is crude, but it is all they can think of to do.

For many children, throwing a tantrum seems like a last-ditch effort, after they have tried other ways to get attention and have failed. Unfortunately, of course, such behavior often generates exactly the opposite result from what the child wants and needs.

At boarding school, in my disheveled, frantic state, I was taken to another nun, who told me that if I acted that way again, I would go crazy. I withdrew emotionally and didn't bring those feelings out again, in any form, until I was twenty-one years old.

Looking back, I see that in throwing that tantrum I was risking ridicule, rejection, criticism, people judging me as unstable and immature—all so that I could demonstrate how badly I needed to show my pain.

I was frightened and overwhelmed by those painful feelings. When I was told that my behavior was crazy, in effect I stonewalled my feelings, shutting them up again and not dealing with them for a long, long time.

Children give us many opportunities, with this kind of behavior, to see inside them. I know the mother of a five-year-old boy who found such an opportunity, which some parents might have missed. Her child had recently had eye surgery to correct drooping lids and was recovering well. His vision had improved and he was healing nicely, but he was going around the house whimpering and whining, irritating his mother. "What I really wanted to do," she told me, "was put him in the garbage can and close the lid." Naturally, she did not, but realizing that something was brewing inside him, took him onto her lap and held him close. He started to cry. She said, "You know, I bet you still have some feelings left over from going through surgery, don't you?" And he started to tell her about how scared he had been, how he had been put to sleep before the end of the movie he had been watching, and all sorts of leftover angers and frights. He needed to complain and to get those fears out. Instead of doing that initially, because he didn't know how, he had whimpered and whined. His mother, a sensitive woman, had given him the chance he needed. It only took that little bit of attention, applied in the right direction, and he returned to his normal happy self.

All that mother did was make a simple gesture, which was the opposite of what her irritation with him told her to do. She was able to look beyond her own inconveni-

ence, her own irritation, into her child, to see the reason
behind his behavior. She let herself concentrate on him.
In the process, she allowed herself to be what she wanted
most of all to be, which was a loving, understanding
mother.

These are only two examples of how children show us
what is going on inside them. Every child gives us dozens
of clues each day. All we need to do is take the time and
energy to look.

What Does Your Child's Behavior Mean?

Throwing Tantrums

Tantrums are caused by pressure that builds up and
bursts forth. In children seven years old and older, tantrums are different from those in younger children. In
two-and three-year-olds, a tantrum is a response to the
need for independence. It is the statement, "I don't want
to do it your way; I want to do it my way." This is develop-
mentally appropriate (although it may not be very pleasant in the middle of a supermarket). But in older children,
it represents more clearly a response to stress and frustration. It means the child is not getting the attention or the
reassurance that he needs. Children who throw tantrums
may be frightened about something that is not being recognized or attended to. It is an attempt, crude as it may
be, to say they need attention. The tantrum represents a
revving up of their demand for attention; if they have
tried other, subtler means and have not been successful,
they may resort to tantrums.

Crying

If you study the pattern of your child's crying, you will
probably see that he cries when he has an audience. A

child may hurt himself at school or on a playground and not begin crying until he gets home and starts telling his mother his story. It may be hours since the incident occurred. Tears are a way of letting somebody know that you are hurting, that you are moved, or that something important is happening to you emotionally. Tears, like tantrums, are a way of going public with feelings.

Pouting

Have you ever noticed how difficult it is to ignore a pouting child? You know that look! The head is tilted down and you are looked at from beneath the lids or out of the corners of the eyes. Even if the pouter has his eyes lowered, he looks around to see if anyone is noticing. The back is rounded in a posture of defeat, a posture that says, "Feel sorry for me." Younger children may poke out their lower lip.

Children who pout tend to be clingy; they're always around. They don't disappear with their misery, but they stand right there, waiting for you to look at them, to notice how unhappy they are. They want you to read their faces. They want attention but are unable to ask for it.

This behavior is irritating to be around. You feel manipulated by pouting children because you feel that they are not being straight with you about what is bothering them.

But pouting is merely another primitive way of getting attention. It is a way of saying, "I didn't get my way and I'm angry about it. I'm going to be sullen and quiet, and if I give you an answer at all to your question, it's going to be a one-word answer. I'm going to make it impossible for you not to know that I don't like what you did!"

Nagging and Whining

We all know kids who whine and whimper in a tone of voice that just about drives us crazy. These kids have

probably tried everything else they could think of to get
their parents' attention. Failing, they resort to one of the
least sophisticated methods of being heard. Like pouting
children, these are children who feel ignored. Their parents may be paying attention to them "out of the corners
of their ears." The parents may say they listen to their
children, but in reality they are frequently distracted,
only half listening.

For these children, in many ways life isn't working
right. They are constantly being disappointed. Things
that they expect to happen do not happen for them. They
don't know how to be successful at getting what they
want, at being heard, so they resort to whimpering.

Although similar to pouting children, they may be
more irritating to adults because of the grating sound of
their voices, which can fray nerves. In their anger and
disappointment, they make noises that cause them to be
put down or discounted, intensifying their frustration and
beginning a new cycle of whining.

Children who have constant, chronic complaints, delivered in a whiny voice, have something bubbling and boil-
ing inside that they don't know how to express in a way
that will make people listen.

Talking Back

Children treat us, the adults in their lives, the way they
are treated. The more I work with children, the truer I
realize this statement is. Talking back is a perfect example. A child who is barked at, who isn't respected, who
doesn't feel accepted, behaves the same way with his parents. He is disrespectful and nonaccepting. He is saying,
"I am treating you the way I experience you treating me."

You know the kind of child I mean. Almost every time
he talks to you, he contradicts you. He calls you names.
Whatever you want him to do, he won't do. He's simply
defiant.

All the children I've worked with who talked this way had been talked to this way. Their parents are dogmatic. "You do this," the parents say, "and you do it now." Children, like adults, have strong egos. They don't accept being pushed around any more than adults do. Unfortunately, since they are children, they don't have many ways of fighting back. Strong children, those who have positive feelings about themselves, will bark back.

If you listen to the adults in the back-talker's life, you will hear the same tone of voice, possibly even the same words, you are hearing from him.

I frequently say to the parents I work with, "When you give love, you get love back. And when you give _____ (fill in the blank), you get that back." This is as true of children as it is of anybody.

Withdrawing

Children withdraw because they feel they cannot compete in the world of people. Previous generations did this through radio and books; now we have TV, Walkman, computers, and video games. Machines, music, and books are nonthreatening. They demand nothing from a child. They offer a world of escape where a child can be distracted from his pains and problems. Children who are TV addicts or who tune out with mind-numbing decibels of rock music are serious candidates for the more adult forms of mind numbing, such as drugs and alcohol.

This kind of behavior deserves serious concern. It is in many ways easier to deal with a child whose anger is open, who throws tantrums or talks back. That child is asking for help and attention. The child who withdraws is often ignored; he doesn't cause problems. He's not nagging or hassling or getting into trouble, although these children often do poorly in school because they are preoccupied with or distracted by what's happening inside themselves. Although they are not screaming for adult attention, they are the ones we need to be most concerned about.

Shyness

Shy, overly sensitive children have a distinctive look. They dress down, avoiding clothes that will call attention to themselves. Their eyes look big and pleading, and their facial expressions seem to say, "Don't hurt me. Please don't say anything to hurt my feelings." They work hard at not drawing attention to themselves and try to look as though they are fading into the woodwork. They are the ones who stand in the back of the line or sit in the back of the class. In the middle of a group, they are the ones surrounded by other kids. They are the kids who do little participating.

These children are careful to do the "right" thing. Their assignments are handed in on time, they are not late for school. They put great energy into not being noticed. Most people receive the message and back off from these children.

Shy children are self-conscious and easily embarrassed, and they are good at letting others know this, so they are not teased much.

These children are often left out of activities and make minimal contributions to groups.

Shy children are frightened. Their fear is painful to watch and even more painful for them to experience.

Stealing

In my practice on the affluent North Shore of Chicago, I see many children who steal. Stealing is a common symptom of those children who feel deprived or ignored. Children who steal want something, usually love or acceptance, that they don't think they will get if they ask for it. In a way, if you understand the twists and turns of their

primitive thought processes, you can see that symbolical-
ly they think they are taking something that they feel
rightfully belongs to them. Deprived of one thing—love
or attention—they feel justified in taking something
else—money or material possessions.

Initially, a child usually takes from the person, often a
parent, whom he feels is neglectful or stingy with love and
attention. It is common for children to steal money to buy
food or other treats, sometimes video games or gifts, for
themselves and their friends, as a way of nourishing and
nurturing themselves. Later this behavior often becomes
generalized and escalates into stealing from stores or
strangers. It can also escalate into stealing to buy drugs for
the same reasons.

I once treated a boy who stole coins, one by one, out of
his mother's antique coin collection. Slowly, over time,
he disclosed that he was angry about his mother's relationship with her boyfriend. He felt that because of her
attention to the new man, he was being abandoned. Com-
plicating the problem was the boyfriend's authoritarian
manner. The boy sold the coins, he told me, and used the
money to buy candy and cookies. He said that the sweets
made him feel better.

Teasing

I have observed two kinds of teasing in children. The
first, between brother and sister, is relatively benign.
This kind of teasing doesn't mean much and shouldn't
alarm parents. Among siblings, teasing is merely a way,
sometimes a noisy way, of interacting. Boys tend to do
most of the brother-sister teasing. Since we socialize boys
into being aggressive and less sensitive, that kind of teasing is usually a brother's attempt to play with his sister, to
engage her with him, to get a reaction. If the sister gets
angry in response, even though she may end up hitting

him, the boy finds excitement in the play. Boys sometimes value this kind of attention, just for the action it
generates.

I wouldn't worry about that kind of teasing in childhood. It will pass with maturity.

The teasing that is upsetting is the kind that causes
pain. You have heard it and so have I, and it can be awful.
I often ask children why they tease each other. The answers are not surprising. In this world, the rule is "survival of the fittest." Teasing is a way of putting people
down. If I put you down, then that in some crazy way
makes me feel better about myself. We adults do this to
each other, and children are no different from us, only
less sophisticated.

Especially in the middle-school-age years, children feel
threatened by anything that makes them feel different.
Therefore, they recognize, as if by radar, anything in another child that makes him different. The psychological
term for this is "projection."

Children who feel insecure and frightened inside about
their own self-importance are the ones who tease other
children. The children about whom we should worry are
the ones who go up to another child on the playground
and say, "Hah, hah, your mom's an alcoholic"; or "Hah,
hah, you're an orphan now, 'cause your mom died."

The children who tease about these sad and frightening
events are those who are afraid of having them happen to
themselves. They are projecting their own fear onto another child, putting the other child in a "one-down" position, making themselves feel as if they are stronger,
therefore better, than he.

This is, of course, not a healthy way of dealing with
stress and anxiety. The child who indulges in hostile teasing is in trouble. He needs help in order to understand
why he is frightened.

Blaming

Children who blame are frightened. They cannot, or do not want to, take responsibility for what they did. They want you to believe that what they did was someone else's fault.

This is another warning signal that there is something going on in a child that is scaring him. He is doing things that he doesn't have control over or that he doesn't want to take responsibility for.

That child needs to be challenged, in a loving way, to understand what those things are. It is important that if a child does something wrong, he face the consequences. He should not be supported or reinforced for blaming someone else.

Blaming is a way of avoiding guilt and punishment and of staying out of trouble, but it is not a healthy way. By blaming someone else, the child "sets up" that other person. The motive may be jealousy (you see this often among brothers and sisters). The blaming child is saying, "See, he's not better than I am. He gets into trouble, too. He's just as bad as I am."

Although this behavior is less unacceptable in young children, because they usually are doing it to protect themselves, in older kids it is a sign of poor self-esteem. It's a bell signaling that something is amiss.

Lying

This is another behavior pattern that I see often in my work with children. Most parents see it, too. It's important that we understand what it means.

The very word *lying* is loaded with pejorative content. I don't even like to use the word, because it can be so damaging on a long-term basis. People feel strongly about honesty, as they should, of course, but the strength of that feeling often gets in the way of recognizing the motivation for this behavior in children. It is so easy to put labels on kids, and "liar" is one of the most destructive. Children can easily be led into believing this evaluation of themselves and, like the labels "dummy" and "stupid," "liar" can stay with a child, inside, for life.

But children don't "lie." At least not in the way you or I do.

Let's define, then, the kind of "lying" that children do. I have observed three types.

1. Distorting.   Children distort facts or events in a crude attempt to change reality in order to protect themselves. They tell you what they think you want to hear, under the assumption—sometimes correct—that you don't want to hear the truth.

A child who hasn't done his homework, for example, will tell you that he did do his homework. Or he may tell you a whopper—a big dog ate his homework as he was walking to school. In reality, he may have been distracted, he may not have felt like doing it, or a friend may have called him and used up the time he had set aside for homework. It is hard for him to admit that he didn't do what he was supposed to do. He knows that home work is something you expect of him. So when he tells you that he did it, he is only telling you what you want to hear.

He hopes to get away with it, and sometimes he does. Some kids whose parents don't bother or don't want to delve more deeply get used to getting away with telling them what they want to hear. Sometimes it becomes an easy way out, but usually, as life gets more complicated, most children become adept at learning what realistically can be distorted and what cannot. They learn the ways of "the little white lie," which forms a part of many adult social and business patterns. Thus, they become adults, basically honest but socialized.

Children who distort often and seriously, however, who repeatedly tell you things they think you want to hear, need to be given attention. They aren't feeling good about their relationship to you, and you need to do something about that.

2. Exaggerating.   This is common among young children, who have a difficult time knowing what is real and what is not. Young children normally do some "magical" thinking. They make things up. As children grow older, their need to fantasize and exaggerate grows less unless they feel poorly about themselves. Then they need to do this as a way of puffing themselves up, making themselves look or seem better than they think they are. These are children who are often ashamed of themselves or their families.

I see children exaggerating about what their fathers do for a living as a way of making themselves feel important. Unfortunately, as in other cases of vulnerable behavior, some of these kids are receiving modeling from their parents. Children, we must remember, echo what they hear. Many of the parents, too, puff themselves up about matters of money, status, or whatever seems important to them.

Children who exaggerate lose their credibility among their friends and are often laughed at, with, "Oh, here comes another story." Received this way, they feel put down and as though they need to come up with something even bigger, to climb on top again, in order to feel good about themselves. They can become caught in a trap of their own making—the "tangled web" that Shakespeare talked about, "when . . . we practice to deceive."

Exaggerating, too, is a warning sign that something is wrong and needs attention.

*3. Storytelling.*You see this most often in younger children, less in older kids. It is another device the child uses to try to master a problem. Listen closely to the subject matter of the stories. They will be your clue as to what is frightening or bothering your child. One little girl I know, whose father is a funeral director, did not understand death and was frightened by his work. She made up stories about bodies under the ground, which earned her a negative reputation among her schoolmates as a story-teller. Once I dealt directly with the fact of death with her, what death meant, what actually happened, she was able to work through her fears. She stopped telling stories, and the storyteller reputation faded away.

Parents need to remember that children lie when they are afraid of telling the truth. Being children, they don't plan well or exercise good judgment, so they are often found out. Going into the lie, they usually are discouraged about their ability to carry it off. They often assume that they will be caught and punished. Frequently, of course, they are.

The serious problem with children's lying occurs at the point when, in some way, their disgusted parents "write them off." In their parents' eyes, they become "bad kids." When the children themselves begin to believe this judgment, they accept the fact that it doesn't matter what they do, because it will always be wrong.

This becomes a destructive vicious cycle. You often see the results in families where one kid is labeled "good" and another "bad." One mother I know began this cycle with twins, one "good" girl and one "bad" girl. As a way of masking her own feelings of inadequacy, the mother expressed anger, to which the "bad" daughter kept reacting. The daughter felt more and more locked in by her mother's anger and "bad" image of her. Thus the cycle was perpetuated. Then each time the daughter misbehaved, the mother felt justified and self-righteous, because she had always "known" that the kid was bad. And so it goes.

Passive-Aggressive, Withholding

These are children who are not straight with their anger. They invariably disappoint you by failing to follow through. If you give them something to do, they will do it, but not the way you want it done. Somehow they manage to bungle the jobs they are given to do. They may make the bed but leave off the sheet, put in the casserole but not turn on the oven, wash the dishes but not use soap.

I don't mean that once in a while they make a mistake. Everyone fails sometimes. I'm talking about a pattern of seeming to come through but actually not coming through. This is an indirect way of saying, "I'm angry and I don't want to cooperate." This is passive aggression.

For whatever reason, these children have poor feelings about themselves. They also feel, for whatever reason, that they cannot be direct about their anger. Usually these are children who have been criticized in a way that hurt them deeply, or they feel that, in their families, anger is a scary thing to express. They may have tried being straight with their anger and found that Dad grew so furious in response that it was frightening, or that Mom became hysterical or cold in a way that also was frightening. The message in the family is, "Don't be direct about your anger." Yet this child feels compromised. He *does* feel angry, but cannot express it. So his way of telling you he doesn't like this situation, his way of "getting back," is by seeming to do things but ending up not doing them. He is retaliating.

Kids can be ingenious about their excuses. "I didn't know that you wanted me to do that." "I forgot." When this behavior occurs over and over, a child is passively saying no, refusing to cooperate. You need to look inside to where he is holding his anger and help him let it out in a direct manner.

Exercise

CLOSE THE DOOR AND OPEN YOUR HEART

Think about the times in your life when you genuinely opened up to another person. You had that person's undivided attention, didn't you? That person did a minimum of talking and a maximum of listening, right?

Your children are not different from you. They respond to the same situations in the same way.

Set the Scene—Close the Door: Your child must know that you are sincerely interested in his feelings. You can convince him of that by setting aside some time, closing the door, and getting rid of *all* distractions. Clear other children and animals out of the immediate area. Turn off the TV, radio, or any other distraction. (Sometimes it is simpler to leave the house; you might try sitting quietly in your car in a park.)

The child needs to know that he has your *undivided* attention. Often parents pretend to be listening to their children when they are really reading or watching TV. Believe me, children know the difference.

Set the Tone—Open Your Heart: When you are hoping for your child to open up, you must create an accepting, nonjudgmental atmosphere. Very few people and even fewer children will open up to someone if they expect that criticism or a lecture will be the response.

I once treated an eleven-year-old girl who had un-explained stomachaches for two days. Her father brought her in to see me because she wouldn't talk to him. Within ten minutes, she had explained to me that her stomachaches were caused by her worry over a skating competition in which she was sched-uled to participate. When I asked why she couldn't tell her dad about it, she said, "He doesn't listen to me. He just lectures." Many children feel that way about their parents, and nothing kills communica-tion faster.

When listening to your child, you must look inter-ested and open to what he is saying. Try to be re-laxed and receptive. Get yourself into a comfortable position and place yourself close enough so that you can touch your child. Most children will respond positively to touch if it is done in a loving, non-controlling manner.

Often, in treatment, I sit next to a child and put my arm around the back of the couch. Then when he starts to open up or cry, my arm is right there to put around him.

Your being quiet, accepting, and warm will help your child to open up and share.

You might start with statements such as

"Tell me what happened today that made you upset."

"Then what happened?"

"How did you feel?"

"What do you think about this?"

"What are you going to do about it?"

Don't offer advice unless you are asked for it. Let your child figure out answers on his own, with your support. This will enhance his good feelings about himself.

Road Blocks: Some children have a much harder time opening up than others, but you *must* be persistent and patient.

Do this exercise conscientiously and keep setting up opportunities to listen. Your child will probably test to see if you are sincere. He also wants to know how committed you are to him. Will you stick with this approach until you both feel comfortable and you see results, or will you lose interest, become impatient or distracted, and drop it?

Be willing to sit in silence with your arm around him or just close to him if he wiggles away. Set aside ten minutes and tell your child that you will be with him for that time whether you and he talk or not. Then stick to that ten minutes. Remember, the child is testing to see if you are safe to trust. Even if this exercise seems not to have worked out for you, the next time you sense that your child needs to talk, offer him the ten minutes and see if he opens up.

I find it just as difficult as you do to sit in silence with a child, especially when I know that he is full of anger or other feelings.

Try statements such as

"I know you are angry with me. I would really like to talk about it."

"I know how scary it is to talk about your feelings, because you might be afraid I will criticize you or tell you what to do. I'm not going to do that." (Then make sure you don't do it!)

"Sometimes it helps to write your feelings down. Maybe you need to write me a letter, and then we can talk about it."

Be patient with your child in doing this exercise. The time and awkwardness are truly worth the investment.

3

Setups: What Kind of Parent Are You?

Children Learn What They Live

If a child lives with criticism,
He learns to condemn. . . .
If a child lives with hostility,
He learns to fight. . . .
If a child lives with ridicule,
He learns to be shy. . . .
If a child lives with shame,
He learns to feel guilty. . . .
If a child lives with tolerance,
He learns to be patient. . . .
If a child lives with encouragement,
He learns confidence. . . .
If a child lives with praise,
He learns to appreciate. . . .
If a child lives with fairness,
He learns justice. . . .
If a child lives with security,

He learns to have faith. . . .
If a child lives with approval,
He learns to like himself. . . .
If a child lives with acceptance and friendship,
He learns to find love in the world.
—Dorothy Law Nolte

You have probably seen these words, perhaps on a plaque in someone's home.

Believe them.

Who and what you are as a parent has more influence over your child's behavior than you might like to admit. What you say, your facial expressions, your body language—all affect your child's ability to handle stress. What you say and do may be a cause of his stress or his comfort. For most children, their parents provide some of each.

The trick—and as any parent will tell you, it isn't an easy one—is to tip the balance toward the positive. By giving your child a solid foundation, by showing yourself to him as an example of someone who can deal with life's challenges, you give him the tools to handle stress for the rest of his life.

The atmosphere that you create for your family, regardless of whether that family consists of just you and your child or a houseful of children, several aunts, and a puppy, is what gives your child the ability to cope.

It may sound like an awesome task, but you can do it. The previous chapter was about learning to read your child; it is just as important that you learn to read yourself. You need to know yourself in order to know your child. Day by day, the signals you give, the messages you send tell your child how you feel about yourself as a parent. The good news is that no matter what your deficiencies might be today, once you become aware of what kind of parent you are, you are well on the way to being a better one.

Exercise

WHAT KIND OF PARENT DOES YOUR CHILD THINK YOU ARE?

Perceptions are all important. Even more important than how something is, is how it is *seen* to be. How it *seems* becomes how it is. How does your child perceive you?

What I would like you to do is check off the statements in the following list that you feel are most descriptive of the things you say. We all say some of these things sometimes, so check them off *only if you say them often.* Try to answer this questionnaire as you think your child would. Better still, if your child is cooperative and if you are willing to hear the answers, have your child rate you with this list. Compare your results with his. You may be surprised by what you learn.

1. (D)   Not right now.
2. (V)   I really liked the way you did that.
3. (I)   I don't know. Ask your dad (mom).
4. (C)   What were you thinking of when you did that?
5. (D)   Do it now!
6. (I)   I'm too upset to talk to you.
7. (O)   You'd better let me help you.
8. (C)   You dummy!
9. (O)   It's none of your business.
10. (I)   I hate you.
11. (V)   That shows you put a lot of work into it.
12. (D)   Clean up your room now!

13. (I) I'll make you pay for this.
14. (Di) I'm too busy. Maybe later.
15. (C) I can't believe you did that.
16. (O) It's just for us to worry about.
17. (V) I know it must be disappointing, because I know you really tried.
18. (D) Because I said so.
19. (Di) I can't promise you.
20. (I) I can't take this.
21. (Di) I'm too tired.
22. (D) That's my rule. That's why.
23. (I) What do you think I should do?
24. (C) You look terrible. Go change.
25. (O) Do you think you are ready for that?
26. (V) I'm so proud of you.
27. (I) I can't talk to him. You do it.
28. (Di) Can't you see I'm busy?
29. (I) I can't tell your mom. It will upset her.
30. (O) You'd better not move ahead without asking me first.
31. (D) No, because I said so. You don't need a reason.
32. (C) You never do anything right. Let me do it.
33. (D) Get over here and do what I tell you.
34. (V) You did that so well. Show me how to do it.
35. (Di) Maybe tomorrow.
36. (D) Stop it!
37. (C) I can't believe you did that again when I told you not to.
38. (C) Just what do you think you are doing?
39. (O) I'll do that for you.

40. (O) I am afraid you are going to get hurt.
41. (V) You really are a great help.
42. (Di) I might get to it tomorrow.
43. (Di) I don't feel well. Do you mind leaving me alone right now.
44. (D) I said to do it, so do it!
45. (C) You really didn't want to do that, did you?
46. (V) Did I ever tell you how much I love you?
47. (O) I was never allowed to do that when I was your age.
48. (V) I really respect your opinion.

Scoring the Quiz: Count your check marks in each category.

    D is the Demanding Parent
    C is the Critical Parent
    O is the Overprotective Parent
    I is the Inadequate Parent
    Di is the Disengaged Parent
    V is the Validating Parent

If you checked four or more statements in any category other than V, this chapter can be helpful to you. It can give you valuable insights into your type of parenting. You will find it useful to hear and understand the kinds of messages you are giving your children and to understand how those messages feel to them.

If the V statements sounded like you, once again you have my congratulations. You're doing great! You are the kind of parent who raises the Capable Kid.

Now let's find out how your child sees the kind of parent you are.

The Demanding Parent

The demanding, dictatorial parent gives his child this message: "I am the boss and you are my charge."

The child receives the message and responds in some of the following ways. (Have you heard these statements from your child? If so, listen to what he is saying and ask yourself why.)

"She is always on my case."

"He never listens to me."

"I feel like an object."

"I am a slave they push around."

"I might as well be a robot."

"She treats me like I'm still three years old."

"They are no fun. They don't know how to play or have a good time."

"We never laugh. He just barks at me."

"He doesn't care how I feel."

"He doesn't know who I am. He never asks me how I feel or what I think."

"He doesn't accept me. I don't even think he loves me. He always wants me to be different than I am."

A demanding, dictatorial parent is experienced by his or her children as being like an army sergeant or marine drill instructer. We've all encountered that kind of person, and we've all known the anger and frustration that results from being the smaller, weaker party in a relationship with that kind of person.

How Children Who Have Demanding Parents Feel Inside

The child who has accepted his parent's message "It doesn't matter what you think, I am in charge here" reacts with:

"I need him to tell me how to behave."
"He knows best; I don't know much."

The child who has *not* accepted the message reacts like this:

"He yells at me. I yell back."
"I just blow him off. I ignore him. I hate his lectures."
"I never tell him anything."
"I do things to irritate her to let her know that she can't push me around."
"I know he hates me looking like a slob, so I'm going to look like a slob."
"I know she wants me to do well in school, so I won't."
"I feel lonely but I avoid him."
"I just don't look forward to being with her."
"I hate them."

How the Children of Demanding Parents Behave

The behavioral symptoms of children who are reacting to a demanding, dictatorial parent are sometimes loud, noisy ones, sometimes quietly physical ones, and sometimes a combination of both. If your child displays the following patterns frequently, ask yourself what you might be doing to cause the feelings that these symptoms represent.

talking back
disrespectful attitude
angry outbursts
stubbornness
provocative behavior
sexual acting out

lack of cooperation
acquiescent ineffectuality
frequent headaches

How Demanding Parents Get That Way

It is a cliché but a truism that we parent the way we were parented. So many times I have had parents say to me when something is pointed out to them, "I can't believe I do that with my kids. My mother did it to me and I hated it."

We repeat patterns in big ways, and small ones too. I know a father who couldn't stand, throughout his childhood and adult life, that his parents refused to use his nickname, which he liked, and called him by his given name, which he hated. Yet he is doing the very same thing with his own son and is seemingly unaware of the irony!

When we react to stresses and challenges with our instincts rather than our intellect, we automatically do the things we are used to doing. In other words, we rely on our past. In the area of parental behavior, unless we think through what we are doing or saying, we call on the memories that we have.

Demanding parents are parents who push. As children they were pushed, and now they push themselves and their children. Of course, they are producing another generation who will grow up to push *its* children.

Demanding parents are frightened people who fear that their children won't turn out well. They talk of them becoming "lazy" and worry that they will be "losers." They are people who are frightened of getting close to others and are afraid to be soft. When confronted with these fears, they will explain that they don't know how to do otherwise. Tragically, this is true.

Demanding parents are those who, as children, were

not held and cuddled. They were barked at or over-disciplined. Often when challenged, such parents will say, "Well, I made it without love. He can, too."

Demanding parents explain and justify their treatment of their children by saying that they are giving them the structure and discipline that they need to succeed in life. They are too frightened of their own feelings to recognize that a child's sense of structure and discipline is most effectively developed in an atmosphere of love and warmth. They confuse productivity with all the other elements that go into making up a successful life.

Often, demanding parents are very successful in business, but they are just as often unsuccessful in matters of the heart.

The Critical Parent

Critical parents are demanding parents only more so. Their message to their children is "You don't do anything right. You are not okay."

The child of the critical parent receives the message and responds in these ways:

> "She is always bitching at me."
> "She nags at me until I want to scream."
> "He is so cold and mean."
> "I don't like him and I don't think he likes me."

How Children Who Have Critical Parents Feel Inside

The child who has accepted his parent's message "You don't do anything right. You are not okay" reacts with:

> "I feel so stupid."
> "I feel inadequate."

"I try to do as little as possible. That way he won't
    criticize me so much."
"I try to keep a low profile. I don't attempt many
    things, because then I don't have to fail and be
    put down for my failure."

The child who has *not* accepted the message reacts like
this:

"I never tell them anything because I know they will
    tear it apart."
"I lie to her because I know if I tell her the truth she
    will just tell me what a fool I am or that I asked
    for it."

How the Children of Critical Parents Behave

The behavioral symptoms of children who are reacting
to a critical parent often go unconnected, in the parent's
mind, with his or her own behavior toward the child. Because critical parents are critical people, they focus on the
other person's flaws and faults and don't want to examine
their own. Their children often display

    withdrawal
    shyness
    secretiveness
    lying
    lack of cooperation
    moodiness
    headaches
    nail biting

Why Critical Parents Are That Way

Critical parents had critical parenting.
There are many similarities between demanding and

critical parents. Sometimes, in fact, the differences between these two types are only a matter of degree, for
they share the same personal problems. Both have the
same fear of being close, the same feeling that they cannot
be accepted, that they are neither loved nor lovable.

Critical parents are even more frightened inside than
demanding parents and have an even harder time hiding
their fears. They put a tremendous amount of their energy into keeping secret from the world, from other
adults, and from their children the fact that they feel
scared.

Critical parents are very hard on themselves and are
extremely self-critical. In their minds, they do not look all
right, act all right, or accomplish enough. Therefore,
since they see their children as extensions of themselves,
these feelings of inadequacy spill over onto their children.

These parents constantly fear failure. They fear not
being liked. In order to make themselves feel better and
more accomplished, they want their children to be successful. They "point out the children's faults," they say,
for the children's own good. They claim that with their
criticism, they are trying to "fix" their children. This
harping has the opposite effect.

Constructive criticism, of course, is one of the most
helpful contributions a parent can make to a child, but
destructive criticism inflicts permanent hurts. Constructive criticism is conducted within an atmosphere of acceptance and carries with it a sense of helpfulness. It might
sound something like this: "I really liked what you did and
was wondering if you tried this how it would work, if it
might improve it even more."

Destructive criticism sounds like nonacceptance and
disapproval. No matter which words are used, they tend
to sound to the child like, "You dummy." A child who
hears that message enough times from one or both parents is likely to begin to believe it, and believing that
message makes for some pretty unhappy kids.

You may know some of them who have grown into adulthood and may still, inside their adult skins, believe that message.

The Overprotective Parent

The overprotective parent gives his child the following message: "You can't do it, at least not by yourself."

The child receives the message and responds with

"She never lets me do anything by myself."
"She treats me like a baby."
"She is always around."
"He doesn't believe I can do anything myself."
"He's always sticking his nose into my business."

How Children Who Have Overprotective Parents Feel Inside

Children who have accepted the message from their overprotective parents sound like this:

"I can't do it."
"I don't know how."
"I am afraid."
"Do it with me."
"Do it for me."
"I can't manage by myself."

The children who have *not* accepted their overprotective parents' message sound like this:

"I do it by myself anyway and just don't tell her."
"My mom needs me around, so I let her think I need her."
"I let my dad baby me. He likes to."

How the Children of Overprotective Parents Behave

The children of overprotective parents may exhibit behavior patterns that the parent does not connect with his own attitudes and actions. Some of these are

bed-wetting
withdrawal
stomachaches
frequent colds
shyness
overeating
frequent angry outbursts

Why Overprotective Parents Are That Way

Overprotective parents often say, "I don't want my child to do that. I wasn't permitted to do it."

These are parents who, as children, were given the message "You can't do it by yourself. You need me to do it for you." As it is with their own children, this was their parents' way of keeping them close.

These are parents who frequently hide behind or live through their childen. I once counseled the mother of a three-year-old girl who told me that whenever she wanted to avoid a party or a family gathering, she claimed that her little girl was too tired or couldn't be left with a baby-sitter. The mother hated and feared social situations, so she hid behind the child, using her as protection. The child, as a result, became clingy, whiny, and manipulative.

I have known mothers who overprotected their children to compensate them for the lack of their father's love. Such mothers delude themselves into thinking that they are helping their children by filling in with excess worry and concern for the parental love that is missing. Parenting does not work that way, of course. Such "smothering" makes children weaker, not stronger.

Some parents who truly do not love their children try to cover up their guilt by being overprotective, which they hope will look to others like parenting. That strategy, of course, does not work either. Any parental techniques that are "applied," rather than genuinely felt, are experienced by children with discomfort, which leads to their feeling stress.

The Inadequate Parent

Inadequate parents are ineffectual. They are often alcoholics or other substance abusers. Their message to their children is "I am not able to give you what you need. I am overwhelmed."

The child of the inadequate parent receives the message and responds in these ways:

"I can't count on her."
"He embarrasses me."
"I avoid her."
"I feel sorry for my dad."
"She needs me to help her out."
"He will give me anything I want."
"I can always get around him."
"I can get her to change her mind easily."

How Children Who Have Inadequate Parents Feel Inside

Children who have accepted the message from their inadequate parents sound like this:

"I have to protect my mom."
"It's up to me to get dinner. I'm in charge around here."

"I'm worried about my dad."
"I can't go to sleep until he is safely at home."

Children who have *not* accepted the message from their inadequate parents sound like this:

"I don't respect her and I won't do anything to help her."
"He's no good. I've written him off."
"There's no one I can count on. I'm alone, and it's her fault."

How the Children of Inadequate Parents Behave

The behavior patterns of the children of inadequate parents is often similar to the behavior of adults who are involved with alcohol and drugs. Being children, however, they feel that they have even fewer resources on which to call for help. They may feel even more "caught in a trap." The feelings that the trap is not of their making and that, being children, they should be protected rather than being forced to give protection may cause enormous frustration. They may display

lack of respect
pseudomaturity
depression
manipulative tactics
frequent angry outbursts

Why Inadequate Parents Are That Way

The feelings inadequate parents have about their children are important to understand in order to help those children cope with stress. Inadequate parents are, quite simply, afraid. They are afraid of losing their children's love, of saying no, of not being liked.

They are depressed and feel helpless. Their children's world looks overwhelming to them. Burdened with poor self-esteem in most areas of their lives, these parents find that parenting makes them feel even more incapable.

Psychologically speaking, inadequate parents are immature. As children, they were often pampered or spoiled. They genuinely do not know how to assume responsibility.

The inadequate parents who resort to drug and alcohol abuse have the most serious problems, and so do their children. These are parents who are frightened by the world and its demands, and who cannot, will not, or do not know how to face its pain and turmoil. They use drugs and alcohol to anesthetize themselves from the pain and to postpone doing something to improve whatever is overwhelming them. Their children are in serious trouble and deserve our best, most persistent help. However, because of the social complexities, secretiveness, denial, and isolation in their families, they are usually very difficult to reach, so professional aid is often required.

The Disengaged Parent

Disengaged parents are unavailable or preoccupied. The message they communicate to their children is "You are not terribly important to me."

The child of the disengaged parent receives the message and responds in these ways:

> "She doesn't like me. She doesn't like having me around."
> "I don't know how to get his attention."
> "She is so busy."
> "He is never around."
> "Something else is always more important than I am."

"He makes promises and doesn't keep them."
"There's no place for me in his life."
"There's no sign of me in his world."

How Children Who Have Disengaged Parents Feel Inside

Children who have accepted the message from their disengaged parents sound like this:

"I don't like myself."
"I'm not important."
"Whatever I do is not good enough."

Children who have *not* accepted the message from their disengaged parents sound like this:

"I don't know why she doesn't like me. I will have to find someone else to have fun with."
"He really does love me but is just too busy to be with me."

How the Children of Disengaged Parents Behave

Children of disengaged parents, in order to avoid facing painful truths, may spend a great amount of energy denying what they see and feel. I see this often in divorced families where the father gets together with the children infrequently and where the children know he could make more time for them if he wanted to. It's too difficult for them to acknowledge that he doesn't *want* to be with them, whatever his reasons might be, so they frequently use some form of denial for their own peace of mind. One child concocted an elaborate fantasy life in which she kept house for her father, cooking his meals so his life would be easier. It was heartbreaking!

The children of disengaged, unavailable parents may show these symptoms:

stealing
exaggerating
depression
withdrawal
anxiety
nagging
stomachaches

Why Disengaged Parents Are That Way

Disengaged, unavailable parents are usually people who need to be parented themselves, because they feel that as children they were not adequately loved. Because of this and the bitterness it causes in them, they resent the parenting they see their children receiving from their spouse or ex-spouse. These are people who are uncomfortable with closeness. They feel awkward with feelings, their own and others, especially their children's, and resent their children's emotional needs. The greater those needs, the more they resent them.

They probably did not receive much loving attention from their parents, so they question their ability to love or parent their own children. They are distracted by whatever is happening to them, personally or professionally, and feel helpless to control or direct it.

The world of feeling is overwhelming and foreign to these parents, because they were brought up in an emotional vacuum. They don't know the vocabulary of feelings and the behavior of intimacy, because they have never experienced them themselves.

People going through the trauma of divorce, or single parents trying to make it in the business world, may become disengaged parents if seemingly overwhelming circumstances coincide with their own feelings of inadequacy.

The feelings surrounding divorce are difficult for everyone involved, but the disengaged parent is the one who will not admit to or face his disappointment and anger.

The disengaged parent is distracted by his own problems in his adult relationships, at work, with his parents, with his self esteem. The sad truth is that there is little room in his head or heart for whatever may be going on with his child.

The Validating Parent

Validating parents like themselves and their kids. The message they convey is "I like you. You are a good person."

The child of the validating parent receives the message and responds in these ways.

> "She likes me."
> "He likes being around me."
> "He gives me responsibility."
> "She finds my contributions helpful."
> "I can talk to them. They listen."
> "She likes hugging me and giving me kisses."
> "They admit when they make a mistake."
> "He treats me like a person, not like something he pushes around."
> "She takes me seriously."

How the Children of Validating Parents Behave

The children of validating parents are Capable Kids. Chapter 2 told you who and what these children are. But because we all want to know them when we see them, because they are the kids who are so much fun to be around, let's say what they are again.

    spontaneous
    active, energetic

happy
able to get excited
resourceful
confident
opinionated, but open to new ideas
reflective
thoughtful
helpful

How Validating Parents Get That Way

The validating parents were validated themselves when they were children or, as adults, they have put energy into "working" on themselves so that they feel good about themselves. They have made a conscious decision not to be victims in this world.

They take themselves seriously. They have respect and compassion for themselves.

Validating parents do not personalize the things that happen around them. When they make mistakes, they use them as challenges to do better next time. They bounce back; they do not waste time blaming themselves.

Validating parents are honest with themselves. They know how to have fun. They are playful.

Their children are very, very lucky.

4

A Child's-Eye View of Stress

Now that you have observed your child's stress from the outside looking in, let's observe it from the inside looking out. If you could hear your child's explanation of the circumstances, experiences, and happenings in life that cause him to experience stress, you might be surprised. His stresses might be entirely different from what would cause you to feel stress. In turn, what is stressful to you may not be stressful to your child.

We all have lain awake at night worrying about the effects on our children of the cataclysmic events they go through. We worry especially about those things that we feel we "inflict" upon them—the separations, divorces, cross-country moves that we introduce into their lives. Yet if you could see inside children's heads, you might be surprised at how they handle these major events with relative ease. Conversely, you might be shocked to see that they can be stressed, sometimes to the point of illness or other damage, by the small, everyday things that you and I ignore or take for granted. And sometimes you will find, as I often do in my clinical practice, that children usually manifest their stress about big things through small things.

The purpose of this chapter is to help you "decode" the clues your child gives you about the stress he feels. If you can learn *what* he is feeling stressed about, you can help him address the problem directly. Since we are all, at times, bundles of misdirected messages to ourselves, and even he may not know what he is reacting to, helping him learn to decode his own clues will be another valuable skill you can give him to help him through his life.

Stressful Situations for Children

Children today are under a tremendous amount of stress. They are pressured to identify with their peers, to dress in a certain way, to eat and look like their friends, to talk about the same things that their friends talk about and yet to compete with the very same people. They are pressured to take drugs, to have sex, to achieve. They experience the stress of changing bodies, the fears of separation or divorce between their parents, of nuclear war, and of their own death or illness.

Researchers Thomas Holmes and Richard Rahe have developed a stress scale for adults, which has been adapted for children. Events have been weighted on it according to the amount of impact they may have for an individual, and it can be helpful in alerting us to situations children experience that we otherwise might not be aware are stressful.

Add up the points for items that have touched your child's life in the last twelve months. If your child scored below 150, he is carrying an average stress load. If your child's score is between 150 and 300, he has a better-than-average chance of showing some symptoms of stress. If your child's score is above 300, his stress load is heavy and there is a strong likelihood that he will experience a serious change in health and/or behavior, although it is important to note that many children with high scores do not get sick or have behavior problems. These children are dealing well with stress.

	Life Event	VALUE
1.	Death of a parent	100
2.	Divorce of parents	73
3.	Separation of parents	65
4.	Parent's jail term	63
5.	Death of a close family member (e.g., grandparent)	63
6.	Personal injury or illness	53
7.	Parent's remarriage	50
8.	Suspension or expulsion from school	47
9.	Parents' reconciliation	45
10.	Long vacation (summer, etc.)	45
11.	Parent or sibling illness	44
12.	Mother's pregnancy	40
13.	Anxiety over sex	39
14.	Birth or adoption of a new baby	39
15.	New school or classroom or new teacher	39
16.	Money problems at home	38
17.	Death or moving away of close friend	37
18.	Change in studies	36
19.	More quarrels with parents (or parents quarreling more)	35
20.	Change in school responsibilities	29
21.	Sibling going away to school	29
22.	Family arguments with grandparents	29
23.	Winning school or community awards	28
24.	Mother or father going to work or stopping work	26
25.	School beginning or ending	26

26.	Family's living standard changing	25
27.	Change in personal habits (e.g., bedtime, homework, etc.)	24
28.	Trouble with parents (e.g., lack of communication, hostility, etc.)	23
29.	Change in school hours, schedule of courses	23
30.	Family's moving	20
31.	New sports, hobbies, family recreation activities	20
32.	Change in church activities (more involvement or less)	19
33.	Change in social activities (e.g., new friends, loss of old ones, peer pressures)	18
34.	Change in sleeping habits, giving up naps, etc.	16
35.	Change in number of family get-togethers	15
36.	Change in eating habits (e.g., going on or off diet, new way of family cooking)	15
37.	Vacation	13
38.	Christmas	12
39.	Breaking home, school or community rules	11

How Stress Looks to Children

I asked groups of children with whom I work to draw and write about the experiences in life that cause them stress. The answers I received were as varied as you can imagine, running the gamut from superficial to serious.

Some common stress factors—the things that bother children, which we, as adults may not take seriously enough—appeared again and again in their words and pictures. Here, in list form, is a summary of the children's feelings. By observing your child and assessing the impact the following factors have on him, you may be able to see more clearly what is really bothering him and to what extent.

Stressful Experiences for Preschoolers, Two to Five

toilet training
starting school
sharing
cooperating
being disciplined, accepting no
taking orders
separating from parents
not being understood when still learning to speak
being afraid of strange animals, people, noises,
    situations
routine being interrupted

*Stressful Experiences for Children Ages Six to
    Twelve*

pressure to perform academically
pressure to conform to rules
being teased
being embarrassed
getting angry
feeling jealous
not being listened to
being ignored
not being allowed to do things when the child thinks
    he can
being overworked (homework, after-school activ-
    ities)
competition, sports
being excluded
fights with friends

parents fighting
threat of violence (media and real life)
being left alone
parents traveling
starting new things
criticism
brothers and sisters
responsibilities
report cards
forgetting (homework, to do chores)
being pushed around
making new friends
money worries
tests
missing the family
cleaning up your room
fear of death (own or someone else's)
teachers getting angry
failing
deadlines for assignments
being asked questions in class
being unable to fall asleep
video games
not having designer clothes among peers who do
being grounded
getting off on time (to school, jobs, appointments)
arguments with parents

Special Stresses for Ages Eleven to Thirteen

body changes (especially sexual development, height, weight)
the opposite sex
concern about what's fair
drugs and sex
peer pressure
self-consciousness

Your Child's Perceptions

In order to take this "child's-eye view of stress," some-times you will have to pick up cues and fill in what isn't being said, because it is unusual for a child to speak or to write in fully formed sentences with clear explanations of how he feels. Even children's drawings, which can give us worlds of information about the artist's perceptions and observations, are frequently done in such a sketchy man-ner that they can be hard to interpret. To derive the most benefit from this chapter, take what you read here about other children's feelings and add to it clues from your own child to understand the sources of his stress.

As an example, let me share with you my experience with a little boy whose mother had died suddenly. He didn't and wouldn't talk about his feelings. But he did begin habitually to snap his fingers and blink his eyes, as if he were banishing his thoughts, blinking and clicking them away. This nervous behavior lasted for about three months.

No matter what I tried, I could not get him to say, "I miss my mom." But it was clear from his behavior that he missed her very much. He sought female company and female attention but had a hard time accepting the house-keeper his dad hired to take care of him. He resented the housekeeper's attempts to do for him the things his mom had done. His anger, projected onto the housekeeper, lasted for six months.

His father had to get a beeper to wear so that the fright-ened child could contact him at any time, and he had an alarm system installed in the house to help make the boy feel safe.

It was even harder for the boy's older sister to deal with her mother's death. When people avoided her because they didn't know what to say and felt embarrassed talking to her, she was hurt and angry. She felt embarrassed herself, because her mother's death set her apart from the other kids and made her different. Resentful of people feeling sorry for her, she made her reaction clear, which made others uncomfortable. At home, she resented being asked to be more helpful so that things could run more smoothly. She was constantly striving for her father's attention, but because, like most children, she was inexperienced in engaging adults in healthy ways, she would employ irritating tactics designed to get him annoyed enough to pay attention to her.

Eventually, the family adjusted to their new situation, found positive ways to interact with each other, and moved ahead with their lives, but not without hours and hours of sharing their feelings with each other.

What is interesting, however, and what I hope will be helpful to you in understanding your child and how he perceives stress, is that in all the time that both children were dealing with the devastating stress of their mother's death, that was not what they talked about. It was the little things of life, the petty annoyances, the minor fears, the day-to-day irritations that they railed against.

Think about the last time you went through something that you know to have been a major stress. Isn't the same true of you? Was it the change of jobs that caused you to burst into tears, or the fact that you found a run in your last pair of stockings as you were rushing to get ready for work?

It should not surprise you to discover that your child's mind works like yours.

In Children's Words

Here, in their own words (and spelling), is stress as seen through the eyes of children from eight to fourteen.

I am worried about dying. Whenever somebody I know dies I wonder if they went to heaven or hell. I also wonder if heaven really exists. And if it does and you don't believe in [it] you will go to hell. . . . I also wonder what will happen when my parents die. Will they be watching my every move or will they be six feet under decaying? What will I do when my parents die? I don't know yet, but while I am worrying life is going to pass me by. I am also worried about getting a job when I grow up. Will I have a well paying job or will I be poor? What will I become?

My most stressful event was when my mom and dad got a divorce and my mom went in the hospital.

The thing that stresses me the most is when my bicycle got stolen and I was really mad, then I got scared [about] what my dad was going to do to me.

On January 21, Wensday, was the most terrified day of my life. I didn't know if I could of servived. It was my dad. He was diedly ill. He had diabetes, he was blind and only had one leg! Well that day I came home from school I walked in and saw my mom and her friend. My mom was crying and my mom's friend had t[ea]rs in his eyes. I asked what was wrong. She tried to say it but it wouldn't come out so my mom's friend said it. My dad died! I didn't think I could take it. It was very hard for me. Well it was about 6 mounths later that someone said something about my dad. Well I couldn't take it. I had a temp of 103 and had to go to the hospital, they said I had to see a phscitrist [psychiatrist]. Well I tried it but it didn't work. Well ever since this day I have my dad in my mind every so often but I will servive!

I hate when my hair sticks up.

I realy feel stressful when I come home from school and my sister begins to bug me. Like she gets up and startes to dance in front of the tv. Or she startes to make noises when I'm studing. And when she's very greedy about lending things. (My sister is eight years old.)

Stressful—When I am in a fight with someone, or when my parents fight. I really can't stand it when someone is mad at me. Some of my friends can't get along with me or I can't get along with them so we are almost always in fights. I am also constantly fight with my brother. My mom hates when we fight because she says that I shouldn't boss him around and I can't tell him what to do because I am not his mother. I also for some reason am always fighting with my parents. We can not ever agree on anything. I am usually the one to make up or apologized, even though I know I shouldn't, just so we're not in a fight anymore.

My mom has a bad ear and she keeps getting bad ear aches. She also gets head aches. She is deaf in the ear that hurts. I get scared because I think something will happen to her.
The doctors say there is an oporation but we're not shure she is going to have the oporation or not.
She is so painful she cries. When a parent cries it must hurt alot. I sometimes cry with her because it hurts me as much as it hurts her.
Somtimes I sit in my bed and think how wonderful it is to have her as a parent. And also to have her. I just hope my mom fells much better SOON!!!!

I get upset when my mom and dad fight. Sometims I get so scared they will come upstair and I or someone else will get hurt. My mom gets real upset.

She get agervated when she is upset and her baby cries.

Divorces are hard because your parents split up an move away from eachother. Sometimes you feel bad and sad. But other times your reli[e]ved becaus the fighting of your parents wont happen as much. Sometimes you have to choose between parents. Thats hard! But other times you just go with your mom or dad. Sometimes you feel ackward towws [towards] other children because you feel that your the only one having a divorce.

One afternoon I was driving to a swimming meet. I was scared because we got into the final meet. The year before we came in last. It was my turn. I got on the ledge. I fell off. The starter waited for me. By now I was real embarced. It was the final race and it was for the plack. I was representing our team. I was real nervous. The gun sounded I had a lead but at the end it was close. I waited for the resulets. I won! I got a me[d]al, and our team got 1st place.

I get very upset when . . . I go to school, and we have a test and I flunck it. I get very upset because I care very much about school. It puts me through stress. And when I come to school and me and my friend gets into a arguement. That puts me through stress because I care alot about my friends. A lot of things could put you through stress. Such as when you accidently do something wrong your teacher hollers at you. Or maybe you don't understand and your teacher is mad because she thin[k]s you wasn't listening. It is hard when you go through stress.

I got upset when my mom and dad got devorsed. I realy got mad and hurt. I thought they didn't love us

kid[s] and they didn't wan't to stay around us. I
didn't wan't to be around them and I felt like I didn't
love them, but I did I can under stand now, but it
still hurts alittle.

Danger—blasting area; explosions may occur!
I'm not the type of kid that gets angry often. You
know, yelling, hitting, etc. But when I do get mad, I
bottle it up, quick! But, the bottle is only so large.
When I take off the cork, WATCH OUT! First, I
shut my hands. Then, I clench my teeth, and shut
my eyes tight. Then I tremble, my face gets red, I
count to 10, and let out a scream *so* loud that you can
hear me on the next floor! The other kids think this is
tremendously funny, so what do they do? They pro-
voke me until I blow up again! And again, and again,
and again! This is, as you can imagine, #1 on my
Stress List.

School is stress to me. I was scared because to
make new friends it was horrible the first day of
school.

I have no father. It's so upsetting My baby sister is
dead and my mother never want's to talk about these
things. She want's to be a foster parent. I want a
baby but i'm afraid she's going to take away from me
and give to him/her. I'm on cruches my classmates
make fun of me. I don't like it but every time I try to
do somthing about it people say sit down. Go away,
leave me alone. I feel like being left alone/wouldn't
you? My family is so far apart I hardly know my rela-
tives. It just makes me so upset./ Have you ever had
a favorite grandmother? I have.

I get upset when: My mom yells at me sometimes
i cry but i understand that she loves and she want's

me to do wright. And sometime's i wish i live with My dad. One reason's to push something, or hit my self.

One day when I was five I was in the kindergarten. People use to call me shorty because I was shorter then all my other kids. But now I am in the fifeth grade I am taller then everyone. But now people tell me they are so sorry but I do not call other people that. I think I am tall for ten year old and five foot and two and a half inches.

My most stressful was when I was babysitting myself. I forgot all about my homework and I had to go to bed. My brother told me to get ready for bed. Then I remembered I had homework so I started it. Then my brother came in and said it was time for me to turn my light off. I said I couldn't because it had to be in tomorrow. I was real nervous that I wouldn't get it done. So I got to bed real late that night.

I had stress when my dog died. I had her before I was born. It was hard to just let her die. I was on a trip when they put her asleep. Her name was puppy. Her other name was princess puppy. She was very close to me. Soon, I got over it in a few weeks. Now I got a new dog. So now I have another dog to love. She is not the same, but I love her now.

One day my sister was in the hospital. Because she had scoliosos. She was in the hospital for 2 weeks. She was bout to have an operation on her spine. I was very mervous. I was stress. I thought the doctors would miss place a bone, and my sister would die. The operation took 5 hours. That made me feel even more stress. I was afraid she would die! After her operation, I found out that she was ok, and she would be out in a few days. I was so happy to hear that!

Once I was playing around with my sister, Jaime. I wanted to fight. Jamie said no. This time I didn't ecept no. Then I Jumped, and kicked her in the leg. Jaimie hit me in the stumick. I punched her in the face. Then dad came. I hid in the closet. Dad Said If you don't come out on the count of three. I was scared But finaly I [c]ame out. It wasn't as bad as i thought it would be.

One day my mom said she was going to Mexico! "Are we going to, I asked? "No I'm afraid not," she said. "Why not," I asked? "Because I am going with some of my friends." "Oh." When she left my grandma and her friend Ione came. The first day I really worried something might happen to her. But day after day I stopped worriing about her. And now I don't worry about her when she leaves the house.

I found it stress full when my great Aunt died. During the day I was scared that she was going to die because she was my only Greate Aunt. The next day she die my gramma was very very sad and every one else was too. Are family coulldn't go to the funarl because we were to far away. In the end every one was fine.

I am worrying when I have a test. And I usually wory when I don't get a letters from my grandparents or my friend too long. Sometimes I worry about high-school and my future. I also worry about my parents, because they work very hard. When I was a little girl, I always worried that my parents stayed out late. I still worry about it sometimes now. Like when they go to the movie or to friend's house. I worry that something can happen to them.

Hearing Children's Stress

Whatever you, with your adult perceptions, might assume to be the source of your child's stress—whether it is divorce, remarriage, new stepbrothers or sisters, illness, the death of someone close—it is important that you listen to him, watch him, and go by his signals, not your own.

Not long ago, an adorable blond pigtailed nine-year-old sat in my office in tears. Her worried mother sat with her. The divorcing parents were engaged in a custody battle for the child and her sister. It was astonishing that the mother could be so caught up in her own pain and anger that she could not see or hear her child's pain and anger, but of course this happens in custody battles all the time. "I hate your arguing," the child sobbed at her mother. "It hurts my stomach." The more the little girl talked, the more the angry feelings seemed to well up and spill out of her. "I'm tired of going to all these attorneys and doctors," she said. "Attorneys are for adults, not for kids. I've counted up. I've seen twenty-one people since this all started. I've told my story twenty-one different times and I hate it and I want to stop. You guys leave me out of this. This is your problem, not mine."

That child was screaming and crying to be listened to. Fortunately, her mother finally was willing to do just that. She did make arrangements and compromises to keep the child off the battlefield, enabling the child to pick up the threads of her life and restore the sense of normalcy she was yearning for.

Sometimes it's a smaller but equally intense issue. For example, in some communities, store owners report a constant problem with young girls who bring scissors into their stores so that they can snip the labels off designer jeans hanging on the racks, which they then sew onto cheaper jeans at home. These are not children who are heading pell-mell into a life of crime, but they are kids under peer pressure.

Their parents need to hear what these actions, these statements, are saying. This is how children communicate about stress.

PART 2

What to Do about Stress

5

Getting Started . . .
with Yourself

This chapter is for you, the parent. It is to benefit you, to make you feel better as a person, more relaxed, and happier. It is to help you take yourself seriously. Indirectly, it will benefit your child.

If you need permission to be good to yourself, I am giving it to you right here. Taking care of *yourself* is doing well by your child!

You are your child's role model. You have discovered already, many times I am sure, that children learn best by example. Therefore, how you conquer your own stresses teaches your child more than any words from either you or me ever could.

In the following chapters, I am going to talk about how you can help your child face life's stresses. Since you are the model and the teacher for your child, you can make it easier for him by adjusting your own life so that you can conquer stress.

Besides, you deserve this chapter for yourself. You are a parent, therefore you experience stress. You don't need me to tell you that, of course. You discovered the stresses of parenting long before you picked up this book.

Parents who take their job seriously—and you are one of them or you wouldn't be reading this book—have concerns about their own adequacies. They are faced not only with a complex world and too many choices for their children but an equally or even more complex world for themselves.

One thing I've learned for certain in my work with children is that we have no credibility with them if we live by the old adage "Do as I say, not as I do." This is as true of how you handle stress as it is of any other area in which you serve as an example to your children.

When we study families in which parents or children are abused, we see a pattern in which the abuser was himself abused as a child. These patterns are handed down generation after generation. It is impossible, therefore, to overstate the importance of the example that we show to our children as we bring them up.

This gives you an excuse, if you need one, to take better care of yourself. You not only need to be healthy and happy for your own sake, you also need to be the best model you can be for your children.

I see many parents who feel guilty about being irritable or moody with their children or resentful of their children's normal needs. It doesn't take long to find out that they are overextended and overwhelmed. They feel burnt out, as if they were "running on empty."

You cannot, as these parents eventually realize, give to your children when there is nothing left in you. You cannot draw water from an empty well. So let's do something for you. You deserve it. You need it. And your child will be the better for it.

Finding Out What You Need

I've thought for a long time about what to say to you about yourself. I've decided that I can be most helpful by conveying to you the needs that I have heard from parents over and over again in my practice. They can be summarized as learning how to say no so you can say yes, and learning how to validate yourself.

You can begin to find out what your particular needs are by taking this quiz. Please give yourself honest answers. You don't have to show the results to anyone—ever. They are only for you. This is a personal, private chance to face yourself, and no one will chastise or judge you. Use it as an opportunity to hold a nondistorting mirror up to your own face and look yourself straight in the eye.

HOW WELL DO YOU TAKE CARE OF YOURSELF?

1. Do you feel you are listened to by your spouse or partner? By your kids?
2. Do you get enough hugs?
3. When was the last time you took an afternoon off and visited a friend, had your hair done, went swimming?
4. What do you do for fun? (Exercise just for the purpose of fitness doesn't count.)
5. What plans do you have for yourself for the next five years; the next ten years?
6. What do you do to relax?
7. How often are you grumpy because you are overextended?
8. What are the stresses in your life, and what have you done about them?
9. How often do you get sick?

10. Are you happy most of the time?
11. Are you doing what you want to be doing with your life?
12. Do you know how to say no if you feel the need to?
13. Do you like the way you look? What are you doing to maintain your looks or to like your looks better than you do?
14. To whom do you talk when you are upset?
15. What are your body's signals for too much stress?
16. Have you ever had a professional massage? If not, why not?
17. What do you do for exercise?
18. Do you eat healthfully?
19. Do you look forward to coming home?
20. Are you frequently defensive or argumentative?
21. Are you generally positive or negative in your responses to life's challenges?

After answering these questions, what is your impression of how well you are doing? Circle one:

very well   well   okay   not very well

What are you doing for yourself that you feel good about? Make a list.

Now make a list of the areas in your own caretaking that you can see need some work.

How are you going to work on these things?

Who Are You?

You, the parent, have to be strong enough, comfortable enough, and clear enough about who you are and what you need before you can say yes to your children.

Children ask a lot of questions. That is part of what they have to do in order to grow. They are testers. They will sound you out to find the difference between a parental no that really means "I'm busy, don't bother me," and a no that means "In my judgment, that is not in your best interests so I will not permit you to do it." They will zero in on the difference between a yes that means "I'll buy you a stereo instead of listening to what's on your mind," and a yes that means "We can go to the zoo tomorrow because I like spending time with you."

Once they are convinced that you are saying what you really mean, that you know you are being honest with them and with yourself, that you know what you are doing and that what you're doing is good for you and good for them, they will back off and stop trying to manipulate you.

In short, they will respect you.

But if there is confusion on your part, if they think they can nag you into getting what they want, even, ironically, if it is not to their advantage, they will do it, vying with you for the position of authority.

Part of being an adult, of being a parent, is being in charge. This doesn't mean being the authoritarian drill sergeant referred to in chapter 3. This means simply knowing who you are and conveying to your child a sense of security stemming from the security within yourself.

If you feel good about yourself, your child will feel good about you, too.

The Burden Mothers Carry

Another truism of our psychological lives is that the better care we take of ourselves, the more we validate ourselves, the more energy and room we have for loving other people. We have to give ourselves permission to feel worthy before we can help anyone else feel that way.

I've talked about the importance of being honest and consistent. This section of the book offers techniques for helping parents be that way with their children. We'll talk about listening, touching, problem solving, relaxing, expressing feelings, and learning to make the negative positive. As you go through this section, you may find techniques to apply to other areas of your own life as well.

Many of us do not take ourselves seriously enough often enough. This is unfortunate for any adult, but for a parent, who has the double responsibility of caring for himself and his children, it is even more so.

In my years of working with children, I have met very few parents who did not care about their kids. Many parents, however, carry around heavy burdens of guilt about themselves, with accompanying packages of confusion, and feel overwhelmed by their own psychological needs.

Many mothers, in particular, have a hard time saying no to their children. They feel that life says no to children so much that it is the mother's job to make it up to them. There is so much competition out there, they feel, so many disappointments, that they must compensate their children for the pain and frustration that growing up inevitably entails.

I meet mothers who feel that they must indulge their children or overprotect them to make up for the absence of an extended family or to "apologize" for a divorce or another kind of "suffering" that they feel they have caused the child to experience.

In my practice, I often meet children who are pampered and spoiled. They tend to be manipulative, superficial, and preoccupied with themselves. This is a reaction to the way they are treated. They have not been taken seriously as human beings or treated as persons in their own right. Instead, they are given "things" to assuage their parents' guilt.

There is no doubt that modern parents are under a tremendous amount of pressure to "make it" in an increasingly complex and competitive world. For the first time in our society, an entire generation of women feels pressure to accomplish something outside their homes. Many women who work feel a need to be "Supermom."

Mothers who stay at home often tell me of their embarrassment at admitting that they are housewives. They also feel another kind of pressure as the number of working women increases and their husbands meet more and more sophisticated, assertive women through work. Single mothers feel the pressure of their own often complex and difficult relationships with men, and the demands for keeping ahead of a spiraling inflation rate. It is not an easy time in which to raise children.

Parents who feel helpless against these pulls and pressures, these stresses in their own lives, may say yes to their children when they really want to say no. Mothers may do more chauffeuring, more buying, more indulging than they know is really good for their kids, and may end up feeling exhausted, used, unappreciated.

These mothers do not say no because they tell themselves that mothers are supposed to say yes, that yes means "I love you." They might mean well, but they are not speaking to their children directly and honestly. They are filtering what they say and do through their own layers of guilt and confusion.

My hope is that, as you read this book and apply its lesson to your child's life, if you are weighed down by those feelings, you will throw them off. You don't need them, and they can only come between you and your child.

Your goal is to get closer to your child. Think of how much more difficult that will be if those layers of guilt and confusion are in your way!

Apply the Lessons of This Book to Yourself

You can see from the quiz that you took earlier in this chapter that the key unwritten questions I have asked you to face are: Are you in charge of your own life? Are you doing the things that people who are happy and healthy do?

If you can answer a resounding yes to these questions, then good for you! If not, I hope that your love for your children will give you the impetus to start being good to yourself.

The wonderful part of being around children is that they give us a chance to relive our own childhoods. We can take the best from their experience and apply it to our own lives, sharing some of their joy, their innocence, their playfulness. Or we can watch them absorb the chaos, frustration, and disappointment of their environment, just as we did when we were their ages.

No one is as close to your child as you are. No one knows him so well or cares about him so deeply. Think what license this gives you to work on *you*. Every tiny improvement you make in your own life, any gift you give yourself of esteem, respect, or approval, is a gift to your child.

Armed with the knowledge about yourself as a person that you have acquired in this chapter, I hope that you will read the rest of this book with yourself as well as your child in mind, because even though I have developed the techniques you will find here for children, they are applicable to all of us.

The better care we take of ourselves, the better we take care of those we love.

My prescription is for you to do something nice for yourself and do it today.

6

Just Relax

You know from your own experience how important it is to be able to relax. You know how you feel when you are tense, tight, upset, or overtired, and how relaxing makes you feel better, restores and refreshes you, and gives you renewed energy to face what you must.

We all have our favorite techniques for relaxing, but we adults sometimes forget that it may have taken us years to learn or acquire them. Considering the tension-filled world we ask our school-age children to live in, I think that we should teach relaxation techniques in schools.

Since we do not, and since relaxation is vitally important in helping your child learn to conquer stress, you will do him an enormous favor if you teach him the simple techniques contained in this chapter. They will enable him to relax anywhere, anytime.

Back in chapter 1, I defined stress as any "extra demand made on the body." Depending on the degree of the perceived danger of any particular stress, our autonomic nervous systems release hormones that cause chemical changes ranging from simple to profound. Among the physiological changes stress can cause us to experience are an increased heartbeat, speeded-up breathing, and blood rushing to our brains.

The reason that relaxation is so important is that it breaks the chain of physiological response that occurs when we feel stress. Just by changing the rate and depth of your breathing, you can slow down your heart and decrease the blood flow to your brain. When muscles relax, they return to their normal resting state. This calms the flight-fight response. Hormonal equilibrium is reestablished, and the overall metabolism is slowed.

That is why you feel better when you relax. It is *not* just in your head, it is very definitely in your body too!

The Mind-Body Connection in Illness

Many illnesses are seen by researchers as responses to chronic stress. Although there is considerable controversy in the field of stress control, some remarkable results have been achieved by researchers.

Carl and Stephanie Simonton, a radiologist and a psychologist, work with cancer patients in Texas. They regularly use relaxation techniques as a central part of their treatment. In their work they proceed on the theory that cancer patients, who of course are under tremendous stress, are unable to relax and break the cycle of the chronic flight-fight response. This, the Simontons believe, affects their immune systems' ability to fight off cancer cells. In their observations of these patients, the stress response causes a chronically high level of hormones to be pumped through their bodies, which in turn alters the effectiveness of their otherwise normal immune systems.

By means of a regimen that includes teaching relaxation techniques to these patients, the Simontons have achieved some dramatic improvements.

If Your Child Shows Stress Symptoms

There are many other examples of the connection between stress and illness. We'll go into some of them in chapter 12, but I think it might be helpful here to list some of the signs of stress you should be looking for in your child. By making yourself alert to these symptoms and what they mean, you can help your child learn to bring them under control before they become bigger, more deeply entrenched, and a serious health problem.

The symptoms are:

unexplained aching muscles
neckaches
backaches
pounding heart
frequent headaches
restlessness
impulsive, uncontrolled eating
difficulty concentrating
difficulty sleeping
difficulty staying awake
unexplained tiredness
chronic irritability
irritating behavior
lack of naturalness and spontaneity
nail biting, hair pulling, other nervous habits
habitual picking at sores or scabs

If your child displays any of these signs, or a combination of them, then helping him learn to relax will be another giant gift you can give him. In the long run, and in his life to come, it will do him more good than any electric train, video game, or other material present you might give him. What you teach him will not break or be outgrown; it will last forever.

Children's Natural Methods of Relaxation

Before we go on to the relaxation techniques you can teach your child, I thought you might enjoy seeing a list compiled by some children I know of the natural methods they use to calm themselves down. (We hear so much about "unwinding" with a drink and are so frightened about drug and alcohol abuse among our young people that sometimes we need to remind ourselves that there are many *healthy* young people who use nonchemical methods to accomplish the very important goal of relaxation.)

This list was devised from my work with children between the ages of eight and fourteen, but many of the favorite relaxation techniques of younger children also appear here.

kicking a soccer ball against a wall
shooting baskets
reading
lying down
listening to music
playing my guitar
watching TV
hugging my cats
talking to a friend on the phone
playing video games
working with my computer
watching my fish
walking the dog
walking

running
whistling
talking to my bird
doing a project
being hugged and touched
eating
taking a nap

If you don't see your own child's usual technique listed here, and if you wonder how he calms himself down, just ask him. You may be pleasantly surprised to discover that he is more in tune with his feelings and tensions than you realize.

If you do recognize your child's technique on this list, then the next time he becomes upset, you can gently suggest to him that he practice it. He will be amazed at your insight and touched by your concern, but, more important, you will be providing him with a helpful reminder. We *all*, when we get too caught up in a situation, sometimes lose sight of the simplest solutions to our problems.

Relaxation Through Exercise

Children recognize the value of exercise as a way of relieving tension. Fortunately, they have not been socialized, as so many adults have, into thinking that there is a right and a wrong way to exercise. They don't need celebrity-authored books, elaborately produced videotapes, or health clubs to teach them how to exercise. They have the confidence and wisdom to go outside, get on their bikes, and ride.

Exercise as a stress reducer is effective because it "invigorates the brain" and provides the opportunity to get your mind off what is bothering you. The primary focus is on muscular strength and endurance, cardiovascular endurance, flexibility, and physical balance.

Relaxation and Breathing

In any person, child or adult, who is frightened, upset, or angry, there are changes in respiration. These do not follow a particular pattern and vary from person to person, from episode to episode, sometimes even from minute to minute. Listen to the breathing of your child when he is under stress. You may hear gasps or pants. He may have to catch his breath. His breathing may sound labored, as if he were in respiratory distress, although you know him to be healthy.

The kind of breathing associated with anxiety takes place mostly in the upper chest. Watch your child to see if his collar or neckline is moving rapidly up and down with each breath he takes. Is he breathing fast?

Reminding him to breathe slowly, using the lower part of the lungs, and emphasizing or pushing hard on the out breath rather than the in breath will not only distract him but will calm him down. You will be able to see him relax as he concentrates on slowing and deepening his breaths.

In *Stress and Relaxation*, author Jane Madders suggests the following exercise: "Tighten up *all* your muscles as hard as you can . . . very tight. Then tighter. Then let go and relax."

By teaching this simple exercise to your child, you help him become aware of the link between breathing and relaxation. As he tightens up, he will feel himself holding his breath. As he lets go, he will let the breath out. Although he won't even have to think about it—because this connection occurs so naturally—it will show him better than any words could how his breathing is tied to his tension and relaxation.

A well-known technique in stress management, devised by Charles and Elizabeth Stroebel, called the Quieting Reflex, is a short, simple deep-breathing exercise. Margaret Holland, a respected educational psychologist who adapted the Quieting Reflex for children, reminds us that "when we change the way we breathe, we change the way we think and feel about a situation. Breathing is our life's rhythm. When we breathe slowly, we feel quiet, peaceful, and calm. When we practice slow breathing, we calm down. You can do this any time you want."

The Quick Relax

The "Quick Relax" that I use in my work with children is an adaptation of Margaret Holland's research.

The Quick Relax is practical because it is easy to teach and only takes six seconds to do. I have found that whenever I attempt to involve children in longer, more complicated relaxation programs, their attention wanders and their interest wanes, but they like this one. They can do it anywhere, anytime, without anyone knowing about it. They even find it fun—and it works!

How to Do the Quick Relax

There are three basic steps to the Quick Relax.

Step One: Become aware that you are upset. By this time, with your help, your child will be learning to recognize his own "body signals." He will be starting to realize that his headaches, sweaty palms, fast heartbeat, or other physical symptoms are telling him that he is experiencing tension. As he learns to read his own personal signals to himself, he will quickly grow to understand that they mean he is feeling stress.

Step Two: Smile inwardly and tell yourself that you can calm yourself down.   This step is very important. It must not be skipped. It changes the way your child feels about the situation he is in. Rather than feeling as if he is a victim of the situation and helpless to change or control it, he is telling himself that there *is* something he can do to make it better.

Step Three: Breathe slowly and easily through imaginary holes in your feet.   First, tell your child to imagine small holes dotted over the surface of the bottoms of his feet. This will probably make him giggle. Fine. It may be a silly image, but it's amazingly effective. Next, ask him to imagine and try to feel cool air flowing up through these imaginary holes, up through his legs, and into his stomach. Now, tell him to hold the air like that for a few seconds. Then ask him to push that "stressful air" down his body, back down his legs, and out through the holes in his feet.

Step Four: Go in your mind to that place where you are fully relaxed and happy (optional).   Only your child knows where that particular place is for him. Your mental spot of relaxation may not be his spot at all. Ask him to imagine his place, whether it is outdoors in the sunshine playing with his dog, romping on a favorite beach, curling into Grandma's lap . . . wherever.

The more details he can imagine, the more powerful and effective this added part of the exercise will be. Help him by softly asking these questions:

> What are you wearing?
> What can you smell?
> What does the air feel like on you?
> Who is with you?
> What do you hear?
> What are you feeling inside?

How Children Use the Quick Relax

An eleven-year-old girl I know competes in ice-skating exhibitions. Even if she were an adult, this would be a stressful activity. One day, particularly tense, she announced to her mother, "Well, Mom, I guess this is the time for me to do the QR." She closed her eyes and proceeded, in a few seconds, to calm herself down. The mother told me later that she had actually *seen* tension drain out of her daughter's face. The mother was impressed, not only because the child had thought about how to help herself but also because she followed through and succeeded.

Kids tell me that they use the QR on the basketball court while preparing to shoot a basket. One boy told me that he used it while getting ready to punch his brother. The happy ending to his story is that, calmer and thinking more clearly, he didn't punch his brother after all, which led to his *not* being punished for hitting his brother, which led to his feeling ecstatic about the effectiveness of this exercise!

Children use the QR frequently before exams. Imagine how helpful this technique would have been for you when you were in school. Do you remember sitting down to take a test, looking at the questions, and panicking? Do you remember thinking, "I don't know the answer to any of these?" I certainly had that experience. So did most people I know. Many adults have nightmares about taking tests for years after they finish school.

So you can see what a useful technique for stress control you are giving your child when you give him the QR.

DEEP BREATHING

Calm, controlled deep breathing is the shortest, fastest, most-available tool for conquering stress that you can provide for your child. Train him to use it whenever he has to face a difficult situation. Getting him started with this simple exercise when he is six, nine, or eleven will help him later take his college entrance exams, will stand him in good stead when he is arguing a case before a jury, when caught in a rush-hour traffic jam, or when running for the presidency of the United States!

When you are in a quiet relaxed mood, show him how to inhale slowly and deeply, then how to let the breath out slowly and deeply. Be sure he lets the whole breath out. Tell him to empty his lungs, to feel all the air come out, even from the bottom of his lungs. Then breathe in with him while he slowly fills them up again.

Make him conscious of his ability to control his breath. Don't worry that he will hurt himself. Children who hold their breath too long do so when they are holding *on* to stress, not when they are letting it go.

Uses for the Exercise:

1. After an argument or fight, remind him to breathe deeply. This will help him calm down. Most people, including children, carry an "afterburn" for quite a while at the end of an argument. Deep breathing will allow it to drain away.

2. If you must do something to your child that causes him pain, such as changing a dressing or giving a shot, ask him to breathe in and out, slowly and deeply, with controlled breaths. Fear intensifies pain. If you have given birth, you certainly already know that. Therefore, deep breathing—which decreases apprehension, relaxes tense muscles, and imparts a sense of calm—will decrease his pain. The beneficial effects of this phenomenon will increase each time he does it. As he learns the technique, it will become constantly faster, simpler, and more automatic for him.

3. If your child cries easily, out of anger or frustration, he is embarrassed by this. Teach him to take a deep breath while he is crying. Ask him to hold on to it while he bears down hard with the muscles with which he breathes. This will push the sobs down until he can bring them under control. It won't happen instantaneously the first time he tries it, but it will become increasingly easier. After his crying is under control, ask him to breathe calmly and evenly again. Soon he will remember to do this when you are not around.

Children who cry easily, although they may not explain this to you, feel fluttery and panicky inside. (See chapter 2 for an explanation of why they feel this way.) This exercise helps them to feel stronger and more in control of themselves. It helps curb their tendency to burst into humiliating torrents of tears.

Gradually, deep breathing will help your child feel better about himself, more mature, more accomplished, more capable.

7

Have You Hugged Your Kid Today?

Touching is essential. We don't do it enough. In Western society we are much less comfortable with touching and being touched than are people in Mediterranean and Latin American and other cultures. It saddens me that in our Western world the only time some married couples exhibit nonsexual physical closeness or genuine intimacy is when one or the other becomes seriously ill.

Touching has two very important roles to play in equipping children to cope with stress: it helps them relax and it helps them feel good about themselves.

The importance of touching seems to be continually rediscovered and emphasized anew. A number of books currently on the market specifically instruct new parents on infant massage and the importance of touching infants.

R. G. Patton and L. I. Gardner have published detailed records of children who grew up deprived of a mother's love. The studies show in vivid, heartbreaking detail how these children's physical as well as mental growth became disturbed. One three-year-old child exhibited only *one-half* the bone growth of a child raised in a normal environ ment. The literature documenting connections between emotional deprivation and serious retardation in growth rates is now extensive.

Children who are emotionally disturbed as a result of an unloving home environment tend to suffer from hypopituitarism, resulting in deficiencies in ACTH (adrenocorticotrophic hormone) and growth hormone, the commonest defects associated with short stature. Children in all countries, in all economic groups, react in the same way. If they are not loved properly, they do not grow properly.

Here's how it works: at the time of stress, the pituitary gland produces the hormone ACTH, which activates the adrenal steroids, putting the brain on alert to deal with an unknown or unpredictable emergency. In experiments on laboratory animals, this hormone has been found to stimulate the production of many new proteins in the liver and brain. These proteins appear to be instrumental in both learning and memory. When animals are given ACTH, their brains grow millions of new connecting links between neurons, the thinking cells. These links enable the brain to process information.

The stress of meeting unknown situations and converting them into what is known and predictable is essential in infants' brain development. But stress is not the only part of the cycle that enhances learning. Without its equally important opposite, relaxation, stress can lead to overstimulation, exhaustion, and shock. When stress piles up on stress without the relief of an equal portion of relaxation, the body begins to shut out all sensory intake and the learning process is completely blocked.

Our children, born into a rapidly changing technological world, must know how to handle stress effectively if they are to survive and prosper. We certainly cannot eliminate stress, nor would we wish to, for in proper doses it is an essential component in the growth of intelligence, self-confidence, and achievement.

Touching to Relieve Tension

Touching is one way we provide our children with relaxing experiences. By example and by design, we can teach our infants and children how to relax their own bodies in the midst of stress.

The ability to relax consciously gives a child a tremendous advantage in coping with the pressures of growing up in contemporary society. If this ability is acquired early in life, the relaxation response can become as much a part of our children's natural systems as the antibodies they carry that protect them from disease.

Tension is a word often associated with stress. Almost everyone has experienced "tension headaches." Many of us have had stress-induced back pain. You often see people rubbing or angling their necks, trying to relieve their tightened, tense muscles.

In the flight-fight response to stress, our bodies tense up as a way of preparing for a stressful event. Most people don't even realize how tense they are. If we live under chronic stress and do not relax, we experience chronic muscular tension, which renders the muscles insensitive to increases in tension. A majority of people in such a state, ironically, don't even know they are in it. Not until the tension leads to more concrete symptoms, such as aches, pains, headaches, anxiety, and weariness, is it noticed.

The more subtle signs of muscular or emotional tension include

aching muscles
nervous palpitations
chronic headaches
restlessness
impulsive drinking, eating, or smoking or addiction
    to tranquilizers or other kinds of drugs
difficulty concentrating

sleeping when you want to be awake and remaining
    awake when you want to sleep
feeling tired without apparent reason
irritation with other people and being irritating to
    others
an inability to be natural

Touching and Self-Esteem

Tactile stimulation, or touching, appears to be funda-
mentally necessary to the healthy behavioral development of the individual. Babies who are not stimulated
adequately grow into adults who are not good at establishing full, rewarding relationships with others. Even with
troubled adults, gratifying the need for stimulation of the
skin may give them much of the reassurance they need.
We all have a certain "skin hunger." We must believe that
we are wanted and valued, and touching makes us feel
this way. It makes us feel involved, worthy, and included
with other people in a connected network that says "I like
you"—a message we all need to hear.

Some people are awkward in their contact relations
with others. They are clumsy about having their bodies
close to others and may be reluctant to shake hands or
kiss. These people have had something left out in their
formative years. There was something wrong with the
way they were touched by their mothers.

In a study of the relationship between self-esteem and
tactile ability, Drs. Alan F. Silverman, Mark E. Pressman, and Helmut W. Bartel utilized eighty male and female students. They found that the higher the subject's
self-esteem, the more intimate he or she was in commu-
nicating through touch.

The image we have of our own body, whether we see

ourselves as sensitive or insensitive, sensuous or unfeeling, relaxed or tense, warm or cold, is largely based on our tactile experiences in infancy and is reinforced by our experiences in childhood. The skin of those who have been tactilely deprived is "turned off" to those sensations that the tactilely satisfied experience and enjoy. The turned-off individual may be so uptight about his skin sensations, his skin may be so unused to being touched, that he actually recoils from the slightest touch. There are children too who recoil when you approach to touch them. I call them "prickly" kids.

Studies have shown that psychosomatic disorders tend to develop in individuals who have lacked the experience of close physical contact. When they were children, they missed the hugging, cuddling, caressing and embracing, the rocking, kissing, and other tactile stimulations that children need to grow and thrive.

It is no accident that the awkward people and the insensitive people around us are usually those who have been failed in their need for love, the earliest and most basic component of which is touch.

Being Comfortable with Touching

What you are trying to accomplish with your child, relaxing and reassuring him through touching, will not work if you are not comfortable yourself with being close. Children have special built-in radar systems that can detect phoniness no matter how skillfully it is covered up. They always know whether or not adults are comfortable with what they are doing or are genuine in their intentions.

Being comfortable with touching has a lot to do with the kind of family into which you were born and in which you grew up. Here is a list of questions you can ask yourself to determine your own level of comfort.

If a friend complained of a stiff neck, would you suggest he take an aspirin or hot shower, or would you volunteer to massage his neck?

If your mate complained of backaches or neckaches, would you run out and get him a hot-water bottle or "back massager," or would you do it yourself?

Do you touch others during casual conversations?

If someone else touches you in a conversation, do you accept it or freeze?

Do you or did you participate in bathing your child? Do you enjoy his body? Do you enjoy playing with him in the bath, or do you find yourself anxious to get the job over with?

When you dress your child, do you sit facing him, or do you cradle or hold him while you help him put on his clothes?

You can tell from your answers to these questions whether or not you are a toucher. If you are, you are probably, without even being aware of it, already validating your child. Congratulations!

If you aren't comfortable with touching, start slowly. Ask others for hugs and massages. After you find out how good it feels, it will be easy for you to touch your child. The more you touch him, the more you will validate him.

What can you do to make yourself more comfortable with touching? First, take a good look at yourself physically. The more we like ourselves physically, the more comfortable we are with closeness. For physical closeness to feel good, it is important not to feel self-conscious.

Body massage is probably one of the best ways, and

surely one of the most direct ways, to develop your comfort with touching. It is also a good way to learn about the different kinds of touching and the kinds of effects they have.

How to Touch

1. Your hands should always be warm and soft, especially when touching the skin.
2. The touch should be gentle but strong.
3. Hugs should be firm but gentle, strong and not crushing.
4. Handshakes should be firm and strong, accompanied by direct eye contact.

If you feel insecure yourself, if you feel as if you don't know what you are doing, don't touch an infant or child. If you really don't want to touch him, don't. You may lose your credibility with him. It is better to gain some confidence in yourself first, even a little, and then pass that on, through touch, to the child.

How Not to Touch

Infants and children are especially sensitive to *tentativeness* in touching. They experience it as the adult not knowing what he or she is doing. A tentative touch to a child feels like a tentative handshake does to an adult, as if the person is ineffectual or afraid of being hurt. The minimal contact conveyed by a tentative touch or hug says to a child, "There is not much warmth or strength coming to me from this person. He is not sure of what he's doing.

He's not sure of whether he likes me enough to hug or hold me."

A hug or hold that is experienced by a child as *suffocating* lasts longer than is comfortable. The child feels leaned on, as though he were holding up the adult, rather than himself being held or comforted. A suffocating touch feels overwhelming. It is too strong, making the child feel the adult's neediness.

In *controlling* touches or hugs, the child feels anger and hostility from the adult, which is particularly frustrating when it goes under the guise of love and approval. A controlling hug is often given for something that the child does of which the parent approves, rather than for what the child is. It is given as a contingency for pleasing the parent and feels awkward and uncomfortable. Controlling touchers are themselves uncomfortable, so that the touches or hugs are rough, rather than gentle. They almost, or may actually, hurt.

Age-Related Touching

With young children, we have endless opportunities for gentle, loving, reassuring touching by means of bathing and clothing them.

A technique to which small children respond is a soft, warmed towel after a bath. The towel can be prepared in a dryer or over a heater in the bathroom. Wrapping the child in the towel, then rubbing and patting him dry is a pleasurable experience.

When dressing a child, touch and smooth the clothes on his body. Tell the child how good it feels to touch him, how soft and cuddly his body feels.

Children really love clean, warm pajamas right out of the dryer—another way a parent can say "I love you."

When a frightening or upsetting thing happens to a child—school failure, a fight on the playground, or a scraped knee—you have an opportunity to soothe the child and to make contact with a reassuring hug or hold.

When holding a child who is upset, pull him close and rub his head or back to calm him down. Make your strokes even and soft. Be firm. You will feel the child begin to relax. Continue stroking until you sense all the tension drain out of the child's body. A soft kiss on the child's head, forehead, or cheek is a lovely way to end this hold. After the child has calmed down, *then* talk over the experience and work on solving the problem.

Tickling

Tickling, if it is done properly, is a good way of being physical and close. It is also less threatening than other forms of touching to a child who is suspicious, for whatever reason, of physical closeness.

With a younger child, ten and under, tickling gives you an opportunity to tell him how much fun it is to touch him. You might say, "Boy, this is fun touching you. I like the way you squeal. It makes me think you really like me touching you."

Letting the child tickle you also gives the child the feeling that his touch makes others, especially you, feel good.

Tickling also gives you the opporunity to play with your child. Children value playing and giggling with their parents. There is a real sense of closeness, an intensity that all of us experience when we play.

Play is probably the best form of stress reduction. In play we can totally absent ourselves from the adult world. We can let go of all those worries we carry around and be carefree, worry free, stress free.

Good-Night Hug

As I mentioned in the first chapter, the time of going to bed is a very special opportunity to get close to your child. Giving a child a good-night kiss or hug is an acceptable and nonthreatening way of being close, but parents often find themselves abandoning that time for closeness as the child gets older.

When children are young, tucking them into bed and saying good-night and "I love you" is almost essential to their good feelings about themselves. As a child grows older and more independent, he might balk at being tucked in but won't object to being told that he is loved. I know of very few children or adults who would consistently reject a back rub.

Some children will insist on exchanging a ritual good-night with their parents. The depressed, angry, or rejected child may go to bed insisting on not having it. Yet he needs the reassurance as much, or more.

It's a mistake to "forget" to say good-night and "I love you." Our lives are very busy and complicated, and it is all too easy to forget to say those things because we are preoccupied, but we can't afford to neglect something so important to our children's well-being.

The Prickly Child

George hates to be touched. He acts as if his clothes don't fit. He seems to be encased in a suit of armor that he can't get out of. He doesn't respond to gestures of love or warmth. To others he appears like a cold fish, passive and indifferent. He even feels that way to himself. Yet in every individual, in every child, no matter how prickly, is a loving creature struggling to get out. There is such a creature in George. The trick is to find a way to penetrate the armor.

Looking for Opportunities to Touch

I have worked with many children who don't like to be touched and have found consistently that the stronger the resistance, the hungrier and more anxious the child really is to be touched. It is almost as if these children are waiting to be disappointed or rejected. They seem to be saying, "I won't give you a chance to disappoint me." Such children are very difficult to approach because they give you no encouragement. It is important that the person doing the reaching out not be tentative and not give up. Giving up, sadly, is just what the child expects you to do.

With a severely unreachable child, a pet can offer you an opportunity to bridge the gap of physical affection with your child. A pet can show the child that being physical is okay. You can play with and love the dog and, at the same time, the child can play with the dog, too. While the child is holding the dog, you can rub or pat the child on the back. Perhaps in time you will be able to hold the child while he holds the pet.

The child will register your concern and quality of care-taking as he watches you with the pet. "Maybe," he thinks, "if she is like that with him, she'll be like that with me."

The reason that animals often get more attention than humans, especially from "disturbed" children, is that animals are totally nonjudgmental. Animals pay no attention to your clothes or your profession. They do not care about your looks. They love you, simply and without qualification, as long as you love them.

If the child you are dealing with is really not that difficult to approach but is still unresponsive, then you have the challenge of seeking opportunities to be close.

A pat on the head or a slight ruffling of the hair can be easy and not too intrusive. With a girl, try gently straightening her hair or touching her clothes, feeling the texture and commenting on it. "This looks so soft and feels so soft" is a good start. Helping a child or teenager on or off with a sweater or coat gives you an opportunity to touch. As you slip on the garment, rub across the shoulders in a reassuring, firm, loving way. When trying to get your child's attention, take his arm for emphasis, but not in a way that is uncomfortable to him.

For difficult, hard-to-touch children, the example you set is essential. If you learn to be affectionate with those around you, touching and being touched will become easier and more relaxing for your child. He will grow up knowing that that is just the way people are, and that it is a good way to be.

The Overprotected Child

Children who are overprotected, too, have difficulty accepting touching. To them, the hugging and kissing we have talked about appears to be suffocating and infantilizing. Overprotected children get the message from their mothers and/or fathers that they aren't capable of taking care of themselves or being successful on their own.

Parents who overprotect are usually insecure themselves. Because they aren't sure of their own abilities, they project these feelings onto their children. These children can end up with damaged feelings about themselves.

How do you know if your child is overprotected? Here is a checklist of signs to look for:

> too sensitive, cries easily
> doesn't fight back or protect himself

needs someone to plan things for him or to help him
  follow through on things
needs permission to do simple tasks ("Should I get
  milk with my lunch?")
has few friends
is clingy, preferring his mother's company to that of
  children his own age
is reluctant to try new things
seems upset when his routine is interrupted
complains of not feeling well when challenges at
  school or home arise

If you find yourself overprotecting your child, don't
worry that it is too late to change. Children are usually
wonderfully responsive. Gradually give him more things
to do and always tell him how proud you are of him and
his new accomplishments.

For example, I am seeing a ten-year-old boy who was
referred to me because he "just doesn't do his schoolwork." He gets a great deal of attention and protection
from his mother and is very unsure of himself. Whenever
he tries anything new, he complains to his mother that it's
too hard or boring and she gives him permission not to
continue. This boy experiences failure after failure, and
his mother unfortunately reinforces his feelings of failure
by telling him indirectly that she understands that he
can't succeed. This particular mother is very shy and easily intimidated herself.

It became clear to me in therapy that he spends most of
his waking time thinking about how he can get back at the
other kids for teasing him. He is so preoccupied that he
can't do anything else. His mother's hovering has kept
him from accomplishing things that would allow him to
grow in confidence.

To help this boy, I have devised a system for rewarding
him at school for his successes. He chose a favorite

teacher and I arranged for him to go to her for praise when he does well.

We also worked out a system to help him with his weak areas. He and the teacher look for opportunities for him to lead or organize projects. He has been asked to help a younger child who is having problems at school, and he is taking karate classes in which he is learning to protect himself. When he complains, he is not permitted to drop the classes.

The child is now doing well. Letting go is much harder for his mom. She is trying, by developing new interests and looking more to her husband for companionship.

Exercise

MUTUAL MASSAGE

I developed the mutual massage technique for a twelve-year-old girl and her mother who were engaged in a "cold war." The mother was an intense woman who intruded on her daughter's privacy, and the child was becoming withdrawn and mopey. She complained of headaches and spoke to her mother only when spoken to, and then only in one-word sentences.

I asked the mother what things made her feel good. She said "a back massage." The girl also admitted that she liked massages. So the rule in their relationship became that whenever they felt distant or estranged from each other, either could ask for a back rub. Then the other could receive one.

The technique worked. It gave them an opportunity to be close to each other in a nonthreatening way. Instead of having to ask directly for love or reassurance, each had only to ask for a back rub.

As you can guess, the mother had to make the first move. Soon, however, the daughter started asking for back rubs, too. This proved to be the turning point in their relationship.

The essential elements of a good massage are as follows:

Creating an atmosphere:

1. The room should be warm enough that the child being massaged doesn't feel a chill.

2. A very quiet room with soft, soothing music is best.

3. Cover the parts of the body that aren't being worked on with a soft light blanket or flannel sheet for privacy and warmth.

Being sensitive to what feels good:

1. Ask how and where the person wants to be touched. It is important to ask, "Where would you like to be massaged?" "Are there any places you would like me to avoid?" When you are stroking, ask, "Does this feel good?"

2. Don't give a massage unless you want to. The person being massaged can feel your distraction and your reluctance. But remember that even professional masseurs say that they get a great deal from massaging other people. It's an opportunity for them to relax and enjoy human contact.

3. The back, the back of the neck, the shoulders, and the shoulder-blade area are places where ten-

sion commonly collects. It will feel good to have them rubbed.

If you have a child with a scar, physical deformity, rash, or birthmark, massaging is an opportunity to touch these places to let the child know that they aren't sources of embarrassment for you.The child needs to understand that these places on his body are part of who he is and that he feels good to you.

4. Your hands should always be warm.

5. Children like being massaged with powder, such as baby powder, or with any kind of body lotion or oil.

Don't worry about:

1. Where to start. Try the middle of the back or the shoulders.

2. Moving up or down. It doesn't matter.

3. Pushing too hard. Ask him to let you know.

4. Sexually stimulating the child. We have made a serious mistake by sexualizing touching, so that it has become prohibited. If we are clear that our intention to touch is *not* sexual, and if we learn to convey that message to the one we touch, then virtually any form of nongenital touching is appropriate.

8

Making the Negative Positive

Our problems, you know by now, are not caused by stress. They are caused by what we *do* with the stress. It is our own minds, sending signals to our own bodies, that cause the headaches, the upset stomachs and the remain der of that long list of symptoms we have encountered throughout this book. If there is a single principle I have seen demonstrated over and over in my work, it is that one's attitude is all-important in getting well and staying well. The mind not only affects the quality of life, it can determine the *fact* of life or death itself.

As a psychologist, I have always made use of this principle. From my earliest experiences with sick and dying children, I have been fascinated with the mind-body connection. Therefore, the work of Carl and Stephanie Simonton (referred to in chapters 1 and 6), who treat end-stage cancer patients and who train cancer counselors, has intrigued me ever since I first heard about it. But it was not until I had had a personal experience with the Simontons and their work that I found a way to expand theories about the mind-body connection and apply them for the benefit of children.

Twice, early in my career, I went to Texas to train with the Simontons. I wanted to see and hear firsthand how they put together those concepts that I was finding so fascinating and successful in helping children.

Their work has had a continuing tremendous influence on me. I watched them as they worked with cancer patients and I listened as they explained their results. They showed me how certain personalities and life-styles contributed to making people sick. They showed me the importance of attitude and how, if people could change their attitudes, they could turn negatives into positives, downs into ups, and could help themselves get better. And these were terribly sick, terribly frightened people!

Seeing these principles at work had a major impact on me. If we think we know how people get sick, I reasoned, and how they can make themselves well, why not teach these principles to children? As I watched the seeming miracles taking place in Texas, based to a great extent on the triumph of positive over negative thinking, I became convinced that we could find ways to help even the smallest, most vulnerable individuals prevent themselves from becoming ill. We could enable them to form attitudes that could keep them happy and healthy for the rest of their lives. To this day, memories of that experience give me energy to help kids cope with stress.

Children are not different in their thoughts, emotions, and reactions from the rest of us. They are just smaller, less experienced, and more open to attack. It takes less to upset them. They haven't yet packed for themselves the suitcase full of coping skills that we adults carry around with us.

The inspiration that originated during those trips to Texas is constantly being replenished now. Teaching these attitudes to children gives exciting results. I wish you could sit with me in my office or in school auditoriums and classrooms and listen to the triumph of positive over negative thinking.

The Trap of Negative Thinking

There is a *reason* why it is better to have a positive attitude than a negative one. Looking at things positively gives you options. You can think of ways to change a situation to improve it for your benefit. When you look at a situation negatively, it seems chiseled in stone, frozen, locked in place. All you can see is what is wrong.

Negative thinking blocks you from thinking up ways to rearrange whatever it is you are facing so that it can work for you rather than against you. Your mind cannot rise above what seems to be the reality of a situation to figure out a way to effect change. You are stuck.

People with negative attitudes go through life making themselves miserable. Their actual troubles may be great, small, or in-between; in terms of the way they see them, it really doesn't matter. They think of themselves as victims and, whatever their problems, they magnify them in their minds until problems are all they can see of life.

No wonder they don't feel happy. No wonder they wake up worried and go to sleep feeling sorry for themselves.

People with a negative approach tend to think fatalistically. They feel that their decisions and the directions in which they move are out of their hands. They are simply swept along by events. They tend to be depressed and moody.

Negative-thinking people often complain. They always see the dark side of things. When something is mentioned or suggested, the negative thinkers will immediately list all the reasons why such a thing cannot be done. In considering a course of action, they will first point out all its potential problems or pitfalls. They see disaster lurking around every corner.

These people are usually socially unsuccessful and are even more unsuccessful in love. The reason for this should be obvious. They are not much fun to be around!

The Joys of Positive Thinking

Positive thinkers, on the other hand, appear to others to be happy. They are energetic, playful, and not afraid of their own emotions or of other people's. They like to laugh and they like to hear others laughing.

People gravitate to them. They are good people to tell things to; they seem interested. Indeed, they *are* interested. This is because their positiveness frees them from being obsessed with themselves.

Positive thinkers are willing to take risks. They believe that if things should go wrong, they will find the inner resources necessary to fix them or to redirect the course of action. They have confidence. They genuinely like other people, and, even more important, they genuinely like themselves.

Positive thinkers are popular people, because, just the opposite of negative thinkers, they are fun to be around.

The Importance of Positiveness in Illness

When I taught in the Department of Pediatrics at the University of Illinois Medical School, I spent a great deal of time with children who were on chronic hemodialysis. These are children without functioning kidneys; they needed the artificial kidney machine to stay alive.

I observed that illness strips away an additional layer of defenses from children. While strong, well children *might* be able to overcome negative parents, sick children are just that much more vulnerable. Whatever ability they have to cope with the stresses of life is made weaker and thinner by the fact that they must fight the effects, physical and psychological, of their illness too.

It became clear, as I watched them, that the children

whose parents set an example of positiveness for them, who kept an upbeat, hopeful attitude about the outcome of the illness, adopted that attitude, too. Theirs were the parents who asked questions, who expressed interest, who kept track of their children's medication and diet, showing concern and involvement. The children of those parents themselves gave off an air of optimism. They talked of getting stronger, getting well. Even in the midst of their sadness and worry, they managed to laugh and have fun.

The negative children were those whose parents were negative. If the parents were discouraged, the children gave off an air of helplessness. Sadly, I even watched children die because their discouragement was so great that it interfered with their ability to take care of themselves. Negative and feeling hopeless, they drank and ate what they shouldn't have. I still cry when I think about some of those children who lost the ability to fight for their own well-being.

The Self-Statement Switch

Ronald E. Smith, Ph.D., director of the Stress Management Training Program in the Department of Psychology at the University of Washington, describes what he has labeled the "ABCs of emotion."

Our emotional reactions, he writes, are the result of our interpretation of a situation. He diagrams it like this:

$$\text{situation} \ (A) \rightarrow \text{self-statement} \ (B) \rightarrow \text{emotional reaction} \ (C)$$

The ABC concept of emotion, according to Dr. Smith, helps us understand how two people can experience the exact same situation and have two different reactions to it.

Since B, the self-statement, is equally weighted in this diagram to each of the other parts, A and C, we see that we can change our experience of a situation merely by changing our internal self-statement about it. This is a skill that children, like any of us, can learn.

Jenny, a fourteen-year-old friend of mine, explains the process like this:

Our reactions to our feelings are almost always caused by how we view a specific situation. Whenever something upsets us, we are always talking to ourselves.

Maybe yesterday you and your family were planning on going on a picnic. You have planned this for a week and when you got up this morning you felt all excited inside. You hurried to get dressed in your favorite jeans, and ran downstairs. When you got into the kitchen your Daddy took you on his lap and told you that the weatherman said that there was a good chance it would rain and Dad decided that they should cancel the picnic.

When we experience upsetting or disappointing situations like this one, we usually become angry or sad and react in an upsetting way. If we look at this situation closely, we will find out that when an upsetting situation occurs we tell ourselves about it inside. "This is terrible!" "They're ruining my fun!" and so on. We say these things to ourselves, and it is this self-talking which make us feel bad. If we can learn to change what we say to ourselves, we can change the upsetting feeling we get. This is called the self-statement switch. But it can only happen if we listen to ourselves and think about what we are saying. You may be very upset that the picnic was canceled, but instead of saying, "I hate Dad! They're ruining my fun!" you can change it around and say things like "I really wanted to go on the picnic, but I can have fun at home too. Maybe I'll draw a picture!" This self-statement switch is a very important part of your stress-management program. By changing how you feel inside, you are also changing how you cope with stress.

Now, you must learn how to catch yourself at that self-talk stage and switch the statement around before it makes you upset. Whenever you get into a situation such as the canceling of the picnic, you stop when you find yourself getting upset and ask yourself "What am I saying to myself that is making me so upset?" You will find that most times you are saying things like "That's awful! What a rotten thing for him to do to me!" et cetera. After you have found out these negative things you are telling yourself, the next step is to change them.

By turning your negative self-statement into a positive one, you can reduce stress and feel better.

Although we all know that everything can't always be exactly the way we want it to be, sometimes our insides make us think that if things don't go exactly the way we want them to, we can't bear it.

Usually, we realize that it is silly to think that things will always turn out the way we want them to. If we only can make ourselves accept and realize this fact all the time, we can have less stress in our lives and become happier people. Here are some examples of positive self-statements that can be used in applying the method we just learned:

"I don't like this, but I can live with it. No sense in getting upset."
"Things aren't always going to turn out the way

I want them to. That's the way life is."
"Other people have needs, too. I'm not the
only one on this earth "
"I don't have to be the best at everything. It's
okay to lose too."
"Keep cool! This isn't such a big deal."
"I'm upset over this. How silly."
"So what if I can't go where I had planned. I can
have fun doing things at home."

Remember, you don't have to use these exact
words. It's the feeling that the statement gives to you
that counts. You can make up your own—any words
that make you feel better.

Joey loves baseball. For his birthday, Joey's dad
bought him a beautiful bat. Joey was thrilled. He
took it to school with him for show-and-tell and he
shared it with his friends at recess. When Joey got
home from school, he realized that he had left his bat
at school. Joey didn't tell his parents. He was very
upset and worried. He couldn't sleep that night. He
kept thinking about how stupid he was and what a
terrible person he was. He thought about another
kid taking it home with him. He started to cry. His
parents came into his room and Joey told them about
the bat. His parents gave him some positive self-
statements. They told him it wasn't the end of the
world if he lost it. He went to sleep that night thinking those positive thoughts. They made him feel
better.

One thing that we all must learn to do when we
are doing the self-statement switch is to reward ourselves. We have to tell ourselves what a good job we
did if we did something right. We have to say
positive things to ourselves so that we will keep doing the self-statement switch and keep making our-

selves feel better. By rewarding yourself, you are letting your mind know that you are doing it right. You should be proud. Here are some rewarding self-statements that might help you:

> "Way to go! I did it!"
> "Congratulations! Keep it up!"
> "Good! I'm handling my stress."
> "Great job! It really works!"
> "Wow! I really did it right!"
> "Excellent work! I feel so much better!"

It will take some time. But, if you practice, you'll be doing it in no time. You'll get so good at it, it will become natural. You will feel happier now, and you'll later become a much happier adult.

Perhaps as you read through Jenny's examples, you thought of some experiences in your own life where making a self-statement switch could have saved you unnecessary anguish. We have all mentally beaten ourselves up with negative statements when positive ones would have felt better. We have all slowed ourselves down by focusing on the negative when the positive would have enabled us to get over whatever the problem was and get on with our business sooner.

Having learned this valuable lesson from your own experience as an adult, you can turn it to an advantage now by teaching your child how to make quick, convincing self-statement switches in his own head. You will be giving him a tool that can save him days of misery and hours of worry. This is a simple but effective technique, and as Jenny says, later he'll "become a much happier adult."

How to Deal With Your Child's Negative Thoughts

Many of us, adults and children, carry around unnecessary baggage consisting of "catastrophic expectations." These are negative self-statements that we view as potential bombshells. We fear that if they are somehow given substance spoken aloud, or made to come true, they will blow up in our faces. For example:

> "If I tell him I am angry with him, he will stop calling me."
> "If I flunk this test, I won't get into college."
> "If I don't make cheerleader, I wll never have another date."

Children, especially those approaching and just entering adolescence, talk frequently as though the situation of the moment is forever. I heard a twelve-year-old say about trying out for a play, "This is my last chance." You hear kids say things like "I am fat now, so I'll always be fat."

Because of their inexperience, children have little understanding of time. They tend to view events as right here, now, this minute. Things that adults know not to be urgent are often seen by children as desperately urgent. Consequently, children panic easily.

This, of course, is what makes childhood and adolescent suicide such a heartbreaking phenomenon. We know that its victims were too young to understand that unhappiness can be a passing thing, that tomorrow can bring happiness of equal intensity to today's sorrow.

It is because of this tendency for children to exaggerate their unhappiness, to lose their perspective on what is real or serious and what is illusory or inconsequential, that it is vitally important for you to help your child to learn to deal with his negative thoughts.

When Your Child Is Panicking

There are two questions that can get your child through what looks to him like a crisis.

1. "What is the worst thing that could happen?"
2. "What could you do to handle it?"

When you notice the familiar signs of panic in your child, the wild eyes, the tears, the frantic, desperate manner, sit him down in a relaxing setting and gently say, "Okay, let's talk about this. What is the worst thing that could happen?" Let him spin his farfetched scenarios. Treat his fears with respect. Do *not* laugh at him. Soon his speculations will settle down to something approximating the reality of what might actually happen in a given situation. Let him talk about the worst that it could be. Then, when he has examined this possibility and seems comfortable with it, ask him, "All right, what could you do to handle it?"

Some things, of course, are going to be easier to solve than others. Some of his fears will be childish fears. Some will be true threats to the stability of his life. Needing to lose weight is a far easier problem to solve, mentally and emotionally, than a parent's fatal illness is. But both need to be taken seriously, and the effects of both can be softened when shared with someone who genuinely cares.

Your child's thoughts may sound like this: "What if I can't lose weight? No boy will ever like me." "What if Dad dies? I'll be left alone with no one to talk to."

Once "the worst thing that could happen" is identified and out in the open, it will become demystified. Almost as if by magic, you will see your child's panic drain away.

The *problem* will not have been solved yet, and, indeed, it may be a problem that the child has no control over and cannot solve (such as the parent's death), but when the fear of it goes, the power it has to terrify goes as well. Often merely saying the unsayable accomplishes the goal: it takes away the problem's power, especially when it is said into a loving and receptive ear.

How I Handle Worry and Negative Thoughts

I have my own tactics for dealing wih my negative messages. They have been very comforting to me over the years in a variety of situations when I was worrying about my performance. On various occasions I have been able to

> give myself permission to fail.
> tell myself that I will always have another chance, somehow.
> remind myself that I can learn from my mistakes.
> remind myself about my successes.
> tell myself, if I haven't any successes in this area, that I am just beginning and can't be expected to do well yet.

No doubt you have your own list of tactics, messages you send to yourself that may be similar or identical to mine. Children need help developing these self-statements. We can give them positive messages or we can give them negative ones. Or we can leave them on their own to flounder. Helping them is easy and can be fun for child and adult.

Looking at the Choices in a Hypothetical Case

There are three mental components in the stress process, the ABC we talked about earlier.

(A) situation
(B) self-statement
(C) emotional reaction

Here's a hypothetical stress to show you a breakdown of the ways, negative and positive, your child might think his way through these three steps. Try to determine which way your child might handle this situation or a similar one. Think about how he handles real-life stresses and see if you can figure out whether he is giving himself positive or negative messages. Soon you will become adept at hearing what, and how, he is thinking. In helping him switch his self-talk from negative to positive, you will help him change his perceptions. This will result in his being able to see whole new possibilities in his life!

Situation

"I didn't make the basketball team."
Here are six different ways to experience that stress. Each represents a piece of self-talk, a message delivered to the child by the child.

Self-Statement

Positive Messages

1. "I tried hard, and maybe if I continue to practice I can make the team next year."
2. "Maybe my talents don't lie in basketball. This will

free me up to really work out for the track team."
3.   "I feel good because I did the best I can."

Negative Messages

4.   "I'm a lousy athlete; I will always lose."
5.   "Now everyone will be convinced of what a failure I am."
6.   "Every time I go after something I want, I don't get it."

Emotional Reaction

Positive Outcomes

1.   motivated to try again; challenged
2.   freed up; released from the restriction of one sport
3.   good and self-accepting; proud for having tried

Negative Outcomes

4.   depressed and hopeless; self-punishing and self-critical
5.   incompetent; worried about others' opinions; locked into a sense of failure
6.   angry; defeated; hopeless about the possibility of improvement in the future

Learning to Recognize Your Child's Negative Messages

I know children whose messages are almost consistently negative and who receive a payoff for this. Negativity can become reinforced in a family so that the child becomes locked into that kind of thinking. Not surprisingly, these children, unless helped, can grow into negative adults who spend their lives puzzled about why no one likes them or seeks out their company.

Cory is an eleven-year-old whose parents brought him to me because he constantly complained of being teased. He didn't get along well with other children and had a poor self-image, which, because of his behavior, was rapidly becoming reality.

Talking to him soon made it clear to me that he had trapped himself in a giant web of negativism, which his family had gotten caught up in, too. He would complain about being teased, then in the next breath talk about how he liked to trip other kids and punch them out when they got mad at him; then he would describe how he cried when they teased him after that. He loved being provocative and would do anything he could think of to stir up something.

I talked to his mother, telling her my suspicions about his behavior and what was causing it. The next day, when Cory came home for lunch with another of his tales of woe, his mother fussed over him, as usual, massaging his ego, ladling out sympathy with her soup. Then she watched him longer than she usually did as he walked back to school. As he rounded a corner, where he thought he was out of sight, his slumped shoulders straightened and he began whistling and skipping back to school!

"Oh, wow," the mother said to herself, "have I ever been hoodwinked! I put all that energy into feeling sorry for him. He's got me coming and going."

Since then things have changed. She no longer plays his game. Without the fun of hooking her into it, he has dropped it.

If Cory's mother hadn't caught on, interrupted the game, and helped him learn to look for reinforcement from positive messages, he might have grown up into a very unhappy man.

Another child I know, Andy, comes from an entire family of negative, critical people. He constantly sees the down side of things. If he does well at something in school, he expresses doubt that he can do well the next time. If a girl says she likes him, he says, "Well, but eventually she's going to dump me." He barely acknowledges the positive things that happen to him and focuses his attention, and devotes his time, to the negative. I hate to say this about any kid, but the truth is, he's a downer to be around!

When I'm with him, I find it hard not to get angry with him. If you are a positive person yourself, it is draining and debilitating to be around that kind of negative thinking. It makes you feel angry and frustrated, not only for yourself, but for the person you see doing that to himself. Andy's family is working hard at changing, however, because they are beginning to see the effect that their negativity has on all of them.

Unfortunately, there are many families like Andy's who don't see what messages their kids are learning, people who treat each other with condemnation and criticism, whose concerns are what they can be dissatisfied about, what they can grumble about. And what can you really expect of a child who grows up in such an environment? As I have said so often, and as I am sure you have observed, children learn what they live.

Children must be *taught* to transcend negativity, if that is what surrounds them. Their alternative is to grow up into the kind of insecure, unhappy person whom no one wants to be around. That shouldn't happen to *any* child! And I know that you don't want it to happen to yours.

Or, to put it positively, we want to open our children's minds to possibilities, to make them capable, to help them be people whose message to life is a resounding yes!

Exercise

THE SWITCH GAME

This is a game that will help your child, indeed your whole family, feel better and more positive. It is especially suited for long car trips or other occasions when time hangs heavy and children become cranky.

While in the car with your negative child, announce, "I have a new game we can play. It is called 'The Switch Game' and it works like this:

"I say something negative, like 'evil.' Then you say something positive, like 'good.' Then I say something positive, and you say something negative.

"For example, I say the negative: 'This traffic is driving me crazy.' You say the positive: 'Relax, Mom. It just gives us more time to talk and play this game.'"

Count the number of switches for each player. See how creative you can be. Let yourself be funny or silly if you want.

Negative: "I wish my head didn't look like a ripe pumpkin."

Positive: "It's okay, Mom. We'll have fun decorating you for Halloween."

When your child invents creative responses, lavish him with praise. Get excited. Tell him how much fun he is to play with. Stop with him for a treat, to let him know you find him an entertaining partner. Let yourself laugh with your child.

In a variation of "The Switch Game," members of the family compete with each other to see who can switch the most negative statements into positive ones. Each player gets one point for switching his own or someone else's statements. Put up a chart in the kitchen to represent one week. Before you begin playing, decide on a prize. Perhaps the winner could choose a restaurant in which all the participants in the game can eat at the end of the week.

9

The Importance of Listening

> Sometimes when I wanted to talk to my mother, I would say, "Mom, can I talk to you?" And she would say, "Yes, dear." And I would tell her whatever I wanted to tell her, and when I was finished she would say to me "What did you say?"
>
> —Sara, age 12

It seems like such a simple thing. Listening. Yet for many parents, I have found, it is one of the most slighted aspects of child rearing. It is also one of the most important. Listening to our children is one of the major ways in which we validate them.

It is amazing what poor listeners most of us are. We learn at an early age how to look and act as if we are listening while we are really miles away, lost in thought on a subject that has nothing to do with what we are hearing. We do this especially with children. Many people who are around kids, including many parents, learn to tune out what sounds like constant chatter. You've heard the

143

mother who says, "I couldn't wait for him to talk and now I can't get him to shut up." Maybe you *are* that mother.

Children's talking can be nerve-racking, containing long streams of nonsense syllables, interminable stories, or never-ending and impossible questions.

But children are extremely sensitive to not being listened to. They know when it is happening, no matter what an adult might tell them to the contrary. They personalize being ignored and eventually begin to see themselves as having nothing worthwhile to say.

What Happens When We Don't Listen to Our Children

As I hope I have convinced you by now, it is in the nature of children to want and need large amounts of attention. This is how they become validated. Because this need is so strong, they have to try to get attention, no matter what, developing infinite numbers of ways to do so. When they don't get the attention they need, their behavior often becomes worse. In their bids for attention, they will escalate the level of whatever it is they are doing.

Children who are not listened to for long periods of time may become defensive, uncooperative, pouty, withdrawn, or belligerent. Indeed, they will resort to any kind of behavior they can think of in their frantic search for the adult attention that they feel they must have.

I witnessed an example of this desperate behavior once in my office. It was a frightening and shocking scene, but it clearly illustrated the lengths to which children will go. A mother brought a five-year-old boy to see me because he was biting himself and banging his head on walls. During the interview, while the mother and I were talking, the child made numerous attempts to get her attention. He came over to show her a picture he had drawn and brought her a toy he had found. He repeatedly tried to talk to her. Each time he approached her, she either ignored him or told him, "Not now." Then he started to bite himself. By the end of the interview, he was banging his head on the wall.

You might say to me, "Well, obviously the child shouldn't have been pestering his mother while she was busy." But look at the situation for a moment from the child's point of view. Obviously, he doesn't feel as though he is getting his mother's attention. This was clear even in my office, where his mother had brought him because she was concerned about him. Yet the same behavior she was worrying about was perpetrated right before my eyes, and the mother was totally unaware of the connection between her behavior and his.

This example may seem extreme, but it is not. Children often do self-destructive things—steal, take drugs, fight, flunk courses in school—as a means of saying, "Please listen to me. I'm hurting. Pay attention."

Children don't have the same sophistication we have for using words to communicate feelings and needs. It is up to us to see past their behavior to understand their needs. We must listen to what they say.

On the other side of the coin, in our adult sophistication, we often arrogantly think we understand our children's behavior and what they need better than they do. We jump to conclusions based on our own interpretations, and fail to ask *them* what they feel and think.

In my practice, I've developed the habit of asking the children themselves, very early on, how they see things and what they think the problems are. I gather some important insights this way. Children as young as four and five have explained to me what was going on in their lives. They have come up with some remarkably interesting explanations for what was causing their problems, and more

times than not they are right. I've been impressed with
the answers I have received from even the littlest children. These conversations remind me constantly that just
because children don't have the verbal skills of adults
does not mean that they don't think, feel, and understand
what goes on around them.

Being a Good Listener

Because children don't articulate their needs and wants
in great detail, we have to listen carefully to find out what
they are really saying. We have to establish an atmosphere of receptivity, ask questions, always keep the lines
of communication open.

A little girl I know, when she was six years old, begged
her parents to take her to Sunday school. Since the school
she wanted to attend represented a different religion from
that of her parents, the situation promised to become
awkward. The parents were not sure how to handle it.
They assumed their daughter was feeling the need for re-
ligious or spiritual experience. One day the mother sat
down with the child and had a quiet talk. The mother
asked gentle, nonleading questions, and the little girl responded. What the child said was, "The girls who go to
Sunday school get party shoes. They can see their friends
on Sunday."

By giving the child a new pair of shoes and arranging for
her to see her friends on weekends, the "problem" was
solved before it became an area of conflict.

In chapter 2, we talked about "closing the door and
opening your heart." To be a good listener to a child, that
is all you really have to do. If you turn back to chapter 2
and reread the exercise at the end, you will find directions
for listening to your child, for being nonjudgmental, accepting, and supportive. There you will find how to con-

vey the mood of easy, relaxed openness that you need for being a good listener, the kind of parent your child will learn to talk to and trust.

To help you view the art of listening from the perspective of your child, here's how one child expressed it:

> I expected adults to be better listeners than my friends. I was wrong. Adults are too wrapped up in other things. Big things like running the household or paying bills take priority over listening to an eleven-year-old. But when confronted with the words, "Daddy! You aren't listening to me," he would simply say, "I can work and listen at the same time, dear." But I knew better. One can't do the two things at once. Listening is a full-time job. It requires one's complete concentration. Any person who can work and listen at the same time isn't *really* listening.

Teaching Children to Talk so That We Can Listen

Children often complain that we don't listen. They gripe, in one way or another, that we don't take them seriously, and that is sometimes true. Children may play into this tendency of adults, however, by presenting themselves, particularly in their speech, in a way that makes it difficult to take them seriously.

Children's timing is notoriously bad. They want attention when they want it, not when it is convenient for you to give it. The times when they feel they need attention are likely to be just those times when we are busiest and most distracted, which, usually, is why they need reassurance. Children must be taught to be considerate in this area in much the same way that you teach them table manners and kindness to animals.

Remember the last time that you walked in the door frazzled, reeling from one of those days we all have at work, when everything seems to go wrong at once? Your child raced to greet you and began babbling, spilling torrents of words about what happened to *him* that day. You probably felt attacked, as if your child were ambushing you.

The chances of your taking that child seriously in that situation, of acting in a calm, accepting way, are slim. You are a human being with thoughts, feelings, and reactions, not a machine.

On days like that, in fact, you probably have not even looked forward to coming home, because you feared something like this would happen and you didn't want to feel guilty about not being ready to listen to your child. Let's face it, at such times you just don't have it in you to listen. You have your rights, too, don't forget. You're entitled to silence when you need it, a hot bath, or whatever else you use to unwind from your own emotional upheavals. If you teach your children *when* as well as *how* to talk to you, you will have the satisfaction of being a better parent, a parent who listens.

It's perfectly all right for you to say to your child, "Let's talk later, after dinner, when I feel more rested." But then make sure that you remember to do it!

Bedtime can be the best time to share reports of the day with each other and to share feelings. A child who knows that, no matter what, he can count on that time with you will be "cured" of his need to confront you at inappropriate times with what he is bursting to say. Remember, it isn't so much what he has to say that is important to him but the idea that you take him seriously, that you pay attention to him and therefore validate him. The bedtime routine, even if it occupies only minutes, gives him a chance to drain off those feelings that, if not attended to, can lead to serious behavior problems.

In addition to their often inappropriate timing, children may also talk in ways that are difficult for adults to listen to. They may talk too fast or too slow or they may mumble. Some children talk on and on, often losing the point of their stories, as well as their audience. They may become excited or distracted or discouraged and forget what they wanted to say. To help them overcome all these barriers to good communication and to sharpen the quality of the exchanges between you, practice the following exercise. Like some of the other exercises, it may feel uncomfortable at first, but eventually it will help both you and your child talk to each other with more affection, honesty, and warmth. It will help you both become better listeners.

Exercise

MAKING THE LIST

If you sense that your child needs to talk, ask him to make a list of the subjects he wants to talk to you about. (I think you will be pleasantly surprised to find that he has more serious, interesting thoughts in his mind than you thought he did.)

There are three purposes for this part of the exercise:

1. It allows the child to sit down, relax, and sort out just what it is that is important to him.
2. It gives him a chance to think things through for himself.

3. It leads him to be economical with his use of words.

After he has made his list (and it need not be long—a few items will do), ask him to go over it and note, beside each item, what kind of reaction he wants from you.

This part of the exercise is very important. It will help the child clear his thinking about what it is, exactly, that he wants from his parent; it will give him valuable experience for the relationships he will develop later in his life; and it will lead you to insights into his needs that you might otherwise never have.

Some examples of the reactions he might want to include:

> I want you to listen.
> I want you to give me suggestions.
> I want you to feel sorry for me.
> I want you to tell me that it will be all right.
> I want you to ask me more questions about it so
>   that I know you are interested.

Once the child has learned the technique, he won't have to go through it every time you talk, or even every time he makes a list. But whenever either you or he is having a hard time listening, you can fall back on it. You will find that it becomes easier and easier with time.

There will be many times when your child will say that he doesn't know what he is feeling, that he just wants to talk. Writing out a list of what he wants to talk about is a good way to start a conversation that can lead to a discovery about feelings.

If your child is too young to write the list himself, you can help him. But be sure that the list is in his words and consists of his thoughts.

Here is an example of the kind of problem that might be on your child's mind, and of the response he hopes for from you:

Point: I don't know why I feel blue. I just do.

Reaction: I just want you to listen.

As you sit "just listening" to your child, you may feel that he actually wants a hug or some other form of reassurance that you care. The more you practice this kind of listening, the better your instincts will become for saying and doing the right thing at the right time, and the better your child will become at figuring out for himself what he is thinking and feeling and what he wants. He will also become better at articulating those things. We inject trouble in relationships when we try to impose our own thinking on another person or try to figure out the other person's thoughts. The worst problems come when we assume that we know what the other person thinks and act accordingly.

Here are some other examples of subjects that might appear on a list, along with possible reactions a child might want:

Point: "The teacher yelled at me today for goofing around, and I wasn't doing anything."

Possible Reactions:

Just listen.

Call the teacher and bawl her out.

Feel sorry for me but don't do anything.
Give me a hug.
Tell me that the next time she does it you will
call the principal.

Point: "I'm angry at you, Mom, for yelling at me in front of my friends."
Possible Reactions:
Agree not to do it again.
Agree that if you want to tell me something you
will call me inside or wait until I'm alone.
Just listen to me while I get angry at you.

The following list was written by a nine-year-old who had had a particularly bad week. You can see what was on her mind and how she wanted to be listened to.

Statement	Reaction
I got a stain on my new dress.	I want my parents to understand that I didn't do it on purpose.
I dropped a piece of Mom's good china.	I want Mom not to be angry at me. At least I didn't hurt myself and the dish can be replaced.
I lost something that had memories for Mom.	To know Mom has a right to be upset at me.

10

Problems Are for Solving

Teaching your child to problem-solve can change his life.

As he has grown, you have concerned yourself with teaching your child to use the toilet, to tie his shoes, to say please and thank you. These things are important. Both for your sake and your child's, it is necessary that he grow up to be a civilized, socially acceptable person. But his ability to problem-solve, in the long run, is a far more important skill.

Many children learn, during childhood, to view life around them as unchangeable. They grow up feeling helpless and powerless, like leaves tossed on the wind. This affects their ability, all their lives, to deal with the challenges they meet.

As you know by now, the purpose of this book is to help you give your child the skills and attitudes that will arm him with self-confidence to face any stress that occurs in his life. The ability to problem-solve, if you can give him that, will be his lifelong best asset for facing, and conquering, his stress.

The following words on problem-solving were written by thirteen-year-old Heidi Upman. Please share her thoughts with your child.

Everyone has problems, stress. Everyone will always have problems, stress. The only way to get rid of a problem is to solve it one step at a time.

Often we don't try to solve it. Instead we ignore it, blame it on others, say it's just "bad luck." Those are just excuses. They don't solve the problem. Problem solving is not finding an excuse for why something goes wrong. Problem solving is thinking about the possible solutions and their consequences. To be a good Problem Solver you need skill, patience, and courage.

These skills have to be learned. Nobody is born with these skills. They will be developed as you practice. Patience is needed, because we all have often done things without thinking. The results are usually more problems. You must think things out carefully and patiently. Everybody needs courage to face up to their problems no matter what size they are. Running away from our problems often seems easier, but the problem still exists if we do that. The first thing to do when a problem arises is to decide to solve it. Problem Solvers (people who face up to problems) and Problem Makers (people who don't want to face up to their problems) have many differences. Which are you?

The advantages of being a problem solver are many. Problem solvers look at seemingly overwhelming situations and come up with ideas for making them better. Problem solvers view all situations, even terrible tragedies, as positive learning experiences. Problem solvers do not feel helpless. They do not flounder. They are not vulnerable to other people's control.

Teaching children to problem-solve gives them a sense of mastery over their own lives. It reinforces the fact that they have, within themselves, the ability and the information to handle whatever comes along. It gives them the confidence to know where and how to look for help if they need it. Teaching them to problem-solve eliminates the scared, panicky feelings that can blight their lives.

I remember seeing a cartoon in which Ziggy was explaining his philosophy of life, his way of approaching problems. "First," he said, "I consider the situation. Then, I panic."

You know children and adults who feel that way, and so do I, but it is a terrible way to have to live. Those scared feelings carried around inside are debilitating and destructive. Eventually, they can destroy a person's ability to be happy. That is *not* what we want for our kids.

Remember the last time your child came home panicky and upset? It doesn't matter what the cause was. Perhaps he had been made fun of. Maybe he lost his new wallet or was running a fever and worried about missing a big game. Perhaps it was something serious and truly frightening, something seemingly completely out of his control, such as the threat of nuclear war, fear of being burned in a fire, the danger of being hit by a car and killed. Whatever the cause, the resultant feelings, the sense of panic and desperation, are the same.

Because you are a conscientious and loving parent, you helped your child calm down with words and gestures of reassurance. Now you have a chance to take that parental contribution an important step further. You won't always be there, you know. Now you can give him what he most needs from you. You can help him learn to make himself feel better.

The Skill of Problem Solving

The skill of problem solving is not a mystery. It is simply a step-by-stop procedure for finding and using the best answers to a particular set of questions. It is a learned skill and, therefore, can be taught. You are about to teach it. And, as with many teaching challenges, the unexpected bonus is that you, the teacher, will become more skilled in the process. Since problem solving does, or should, play as big a role in your life as it does in your child's, you will both benefit.

Remember, though, as you work through this chapter, that your credibility is at stake. This part of stress management cannot be a "Don't do as I do, do as I tell you" form of instruction. You must follow the rules of problem solving yourself if you expect your child to take you seriously. In this area, perhaps even more than in others, you need to set a good example.

In doing so, you will begin to drain your own awful, panicky feelings out of your head and heart. And won't that be a wonderful growing-up experience for you and your child to share?

Where Problems Come From

There are three major sources of problems in our lives:

1. feelings inside us
2. other people's behavior
3. objective situations

Your child needs to understand what these three categories mean and to be able to recognize and differentiate among them as sources of his problems. You will find that he is able to understand these categories, no matter what his age, if you explain them simply and clearly.

Explain feelings inside of us by reminding your child about the "self-talk" system in chapter 8 and how we give ourselves messages such as "I am no good" or "I will never get what I want." Let him ventilate some of his own negative thoughts to trace how they might be causing him problems. If he can connect a feeling or emotion he has with the anxiety he is currently experiencing, he will immediately understand and recognize the first and, in many ways, most-important source of problems.

Talking to him about problems caused by other people should be *very* easy. Perhaps he has a little brother who breaks his toys, or he has a baby-sitter who doesn't pay enough attention to him, or his aunt pinches his cheeks and embarrasses him. Even if *everyone* else in your child's life is perfect (a pretty unlikely scenario!), you know that *you* do some things that bother and upset him. Don't be afraid to talk about these.

Talk about how individuals irritate or disappoint us, how people sometimes act in an irresponsible manner, do things that hurt our feelings, or get angry with us unfairly, causing us to feel upset. If you feel comfortable doing so, give your child examples from your own life—a boss who is too critical, a bus driver who is unnecessarily rude. Gradually, he will begin to see that other people's behavior is, indeed, a legitimate source of some of his problems.

Problems that arise from objective situations are the easiest of all to identify. Your child will probably be able to rattle off a long list once you get him started—exams, auditions, moving, traffic, school, public speaking, accidents, sports, parties, vacations, illness, and on and on.

How to Respond to Problems

We have three choices in responding to problems or stress. We can

1. do nothing
2. act impulsively, without thinking
3. problem-solve

In chapter 2, we talked about responses to stress. Responses to problems all fall in these three categories. Whether we like it or not, whether we know it or not, we do one of these three things. We avoid confronting the problem, or do nothing; we attack, or react impulsively, without thinking; or we step back, relax, and problem-solve.

When you see the alternatives written out in that simple fashion, the best choice seems painfully obvious, doesn't it? By helping your child see the choices that clearly, too, just imagine how much wasted energy and unhappiness you will save him as he goes through life!

Steps in the Problem-Solving Process

There are five important steps to effective problem solving:

1. relaxing
2. identifying the problem
3. describing the options
4. evaluating the possible outcomes
5. choosing the best solution

They must all be done, and they must be done in order. Fortunately, they don't take long. Once your child becomes adept at the process, he will realize how quickly he can do it. Like the other techniques in this book, with practice, problem solving will become so much a part of his thinking that he will begin to move through these steps automatically when faced with the challenge of a problem.

Relaxing

Relaxing is essential, not only for what it enables the problem solver to do but for what it will prevent him from doing.

Many children, as well as a great many adults, react to problems and stress with impulsive behavior, be it yelling or throwing things, slamming doors, driving too fast, or writing nasty letters. Whatever the tactic, impulsiveness represents a stressed person's first, thoughtless reaction to his problem, which is merely to react.

This can be destructive, not just because it can result in broken dishes and dented fenders but, more important, because when we are impulsive we make poor decisions, and impulsive behavior upsets the people around us.

Like everyone else, if I asked you to, you could draw up a fairly long list of circumstances in which you, your spouse, your child, or someone else in your life "flew off the handle." You will remember, if you think about it, that the reaction made it that much harder, and more time-consuming, to "clean up the mess," either actual or emotional, and get on with solving the problem. Maybe you can remember a time when an impulsive reaction was so great that it interfered with *ever* finding a solution to a particular problem.

In my practice, I have encountered many people who have trouble expressing or feeling comfortable with their own anger because their mothers and/or fathers were so explosive that their behavior terrorized them. Some people have arranged their lives so that they work as peacemakers, including some well-known clergymen and mental-health professionals, because they came from families where stress was handled in destructive, damaging ways. They have gone through adult life, some have told me, trying to "fix" what frustrated them as children.

The children I see in my practice who explode with frequency are in constant trouble because of their tempers. Often, as they get older, instead of getting better, they get worse. If a teacher reprimands them, their first reaction is to talk back, which they do. Then they get into trouble for talking back. And, because teachers don't have time to analyze why every child who misbehaves does so, it doesn't take long for such a kid to be labeled a "troublemaker," giving him an additional, intense problem and area of stress with which he has to deal. And so the circle continues.

This is a perfect opportunity to remind your child of how to use the Quick Relax. To review that technique, turn back to chapter 6. It takes only seconds to do and calms him down so that he can think clearly. It prevents him from reacting to a problem in an impulsive, destructive manner, and as he relaxes, his mind will clear and he will be able to make decisions more rationally.

Identifying the Problem

Identifying the problem can be difficult, but your child's chances of doing this are enormously improved if he is calm and thinking clearly. Some problems are clearcut and obvious, such as flunking a test, not being asked to a party, not developing as quickly as other girls, or being afraid of a new school and of not knowing the kids there.

Some are more subtle and will be more difficult to identify: being worried about his mom's new boyfriend, worrying he won't be liked by other kids, or worrying that he's not athletic enough to please his dad.

To illustrate the problem-solving process, I will use a relatively simple problem as the kind of thing that could be troubling your child. Please bear in mind that the *process* is the same whether the problem is an everyday small one like this or a major one that your child thinks might affect his entire future.

The problem: "Whenever I try to talk to Laurie, she ignores me."

Here are some useful questions for your child to ask when he is trying to identify the problem.

When did I start feeling upset? When did I first start getting a headache, neckache, or stomachache, which I have learned are my clues that I am upset?

What are the facts? How often have I tried to talk to her? What do I mean by "trying" to talk to her? What does Laurie do that makes me feel she doesn't like me?

Am I sure I have observed her behavior correctly? Who else can I ask for an opinion, to check his observation against mine? What is another person's point of view? Is there an interpretation other than my own that I should be considering? Perhaps a friend might tell me that when I talked to Laurie, it wasn't clear from the way I talked that I was interested in her. Perhaps another person might tell me that Laurie is shy. Perhaps another person might agree that Laurie is indeed ignoring me. Whatever I hear from another person is his *opinion*, but if it makes sense, it is worth hearing.

Describing the Options

Have your child list *all* his options, including those that he knows will not work. It is necessary to examine the outcomes of wrong choices, because as soon as they are brought out into the open and examined as possibilities,

they lose their magic power to frighten. Earlier we referred to catastrophic expectations, where it is necessary
to force the quesion "What's the worst possible thing that
could happen?" Getting those fears out in the open always
helps.

This system of listing *all* possibilities in a given situation
is called, in more sophisticated worlds than your child's,
"brainstorming." Big business has used this technique for
years with tremendous success.

For the problem "Laurie is ignoring me," some possible options are

1. I can ignore her.
2. I can ask her why she is ignoring me.
3. I can continue doing what I am doing.
4. I can forget about her and find someone else to
    talk to.

This seems like such a simple little problem compared with the big ones that people, including your
child, have to face, yet there are at least four different options available to handle it. It is amazing how,
when we sit down to brainstorm, we can come up
with solution after solution for the seemingly insolu-
ble problem, We all become stuck at times and allow
feelings of panic to sweep over us, yet a few minutes
of searching for options will always prove how *many*
choices we have in any given situation.

Even doing nothing is an option. It is important to
know this, because if your child elects to do nothing,
it should be a conscious choice, not a passive decision made by default. This changes the status quo
from something he has drifted into to a decision he
has deliberately made and puts him back in charge of
himself, rather than allowing the problem, or stress,
to be in charge of him.

Evaluating the Possible Outcomes

This part of the process allows your child to speculate on, and examine the consequences of, his behavior.
He asks himself "what will happen if . . .?"

1. I ignore Laurie. Probably not much. Everything will go on the way it is and nothing will be resolved. And I will be doing to her what I am upset about her doing to me.
2. I ask Laurie why she is ignoring me. This approach is direct, and by using it I stand a good chance of resolving the problem. But I'd better be prepared for the possibility of hearing that she isn't interested in me or doesn't like me. If I find that out, however, it frees me to look for other girl friends. Or it could turn out that she would appreciate my directness and my interest in her. It might be the beginning of a nice relationship.
3. I continue doing what I am doing now, feeling hurt that she is ignoring me. Nothing gets resolved, but at least I don't have to risk finding out that she doesn't like me.
4. I forget about her and find someone else to be interested in. That way I avoid dealing with the problem. I also miss out on the possibility that Laurie hasn't been ignoring me, but rather flirting in the best way she knows how. But I also avoid the possibility of hearing that she just isn't interested.

Choosing the Best Solution

By the time your child arrives at step five, he probably will be getting ready to settle on what appears to be the best option. To answer the Laurie question, he will have to decide whether or not he is willing to confront her to find out if she is interested. Once that has been decided, the rest of the plan will fall into place.

Perhaps you will want to "talk" your child through this or a similar problem to see how he would feel about handling it.

Here's another example, just for practice. It was devised by an eleven-year-old named Ellen. See if you and your child can do as well with this problem as Ellen did.

The problem: My mom is always on my case to clean up my room.

Relax: I do the QR so I can think my way through this more clearly.

Identify the problem: I have to clean up my room and I don't want to.

Describe the options:

1. I could continue to leave my room messy and drive my mom crazy.
2. I could ask my mom to compromise with me and let me clean up my room every other day.
3. I could pay my brother to clean it.
4. I could ask my mom to help me organize my room better so it would be easier to clean.

Evaluate the possible outcomes:

1. My mom might have a nervous breakdown, or she would constantly be on my back.
2. Good idea. That way I don't feel as much pressure to clean it up all the time and Mom is happy.
3. It might get expensive and he would be prying into my personal and private things.
4. Good idea. That would help.

Choosing the best solution(s): 2 and 4 seem good.

Remind your child that even after he has chosen a solution, it may not work. If if doesn't, ask him to figure out why the solution didn't work and continue to problem-solve. As he learns this essential skill, it can be additionally helpful to you to remember that the panic that resides inside all of us rarely matches the reality of the situations that we fear.

As we learn to take charge of our own lives, we feel less and less overwhelmed. We lose the desire and the tendency to avoid unpleasant things, because we begin to find that when viewed realistically and head on, they are often not as unpleasant as we thought. As we feel stronger, the grip of our problems becomes weaker.

When we *confront* and *deal* with our problems, rather than avoid and deny them, we feel better about ourselves. We see ourselves clearly, not in a distorting mirror of our own fears, but as the competent problem solvers that we really are. And we see our problems clearly for what they are—just something to be solved.

Exercise

Problem Solving—A Family Affair

Problem solving can actually be fun. It even makes a great family game. In order to "play," you will need index cards or small sheets of scrap paper and a blackboard, a newsprint pad, or an easel.

First everyone does the Quick Relax together. Then each family member writes down on an index card or scrap of paper a problem with which he or she would like help.

Next collect and shuffle the problems and take them one at a time. Or choose the youngest person's problem this time, the oldest person's next, and so on. (Take each problem seriously, even those of the smallest family members, and even those problems that don't seem to you to be serious. Your children may be testing you to see if you will take them seriously. If you do, you will be rewarded by having your children contribute their *real* problems to the game.) Write the problem or situation at the top of the blackboard or sheet of newsprint. Divide the remainder of the board in half with a vertical line. On one side, write "Options," on the other side, "Outcomes."

Throw the meeting open to the family to brainstorm. List the options as they are suggested. When you have finished the options, brainstorm the outcomes for each of the options. List them.

Now, using an index card, each family member votes in secret for the option he chooses and explains why.

Finally, collect and read the votes.

This game can be fun. Children enjoy it because it is positive and helpful and it makes all the members of the family feel as though they are being taken seriously. Everyone, regardless of age, likes to know that his thoughts and opinions are valued and respected.

11

Feeling Feelings

Stress is related to feelings. An example would be you were playing a game about history with your older brother, there were fifty questions and he answered forty-nine out of fifty and you guessed and got one correct. He won and afterward he said, "Ha, ha, you stink and you are not smart." You knew he won because he was older and you had not heard the answers to the questions. So you started to cry and went upstairs and messed up your room. You didn't do this because you were dumb, but you did do it because your brother hurt your feelings.
—Orrin Hild, age 12½

Everybody has feelings but they have different ways of showing them. Take anger. People handle their anger in different ways. Some go home and kick and hit their dog. Some go home and kick and hit their children. Some keep it all inside, not showing it at all. That is bad, but it is just the way you were raised.

People also show feelings in their bodies. If you get mad at someone, you may wind up with a headache. Being sick can wreck your day.

167

Feelings affect how you act toward people. If you are in a bad mood, you may snap at your best friend, your parents, or even the cute guy behind the counter at Burger King. Feelings control you.

Feelings are and were very important to our stress-education class. When I first got there, I was feeling scared, but it came across as anger. I became a rock and I hated it. But I realized that everyone was probably nervous, and by the third meeting had opened up enough to share even *the most personal things*.

Feelings had everything to do with it. I had finally relaxed enough and become trusting enough of the group.

It's very important to recognize, show, and share your feelings. Remember—FEELINGS ARE FOR SHARING!

—Nancy Phillips, age 13

Orrin and Nancy are right. In fact, Nancy sums up the whole matter of the importance of feelings when she says that they have "everything to do with it."

So they do. If only we could realize the importance of understanding our feelings, then teach that to our children, we could all handle and conquer our stress every minute of our lives.

That is not to say that we would never feel bad. Feeling bad, sad, disappointed, frightened, miserable, or weepy is legitimate. Some situations *call* for feeling bad. The key to handling stress is to *allow* ourselves to feel those feelings, when they are called for, to recognize and acknowledge them, then to let them go and get on with whatever is next.

Look back if you will at chapter 1 and read once more the lists of characteristics that mark the Capable Kid and the Vulnerable Kid.

Capable Kids feel, and they know *what* they feel. They feel intensely and fully. They feel negative experiences negatively, but their negative feelings don't last. When they experience something that is frightening or otherwise upsetting, Capable Kids have good emotional recuperative powers and bounce back. When life smacks them in the face, as it does all of us from time to time, Capable Kids get hurt, but they do not get damaged.

Vulnerable Kids, by contrast, have great difficulty giving vent to their feelings. Eventually, and tragically, they reach a point where they don't even *feel* their feelings.

Vulnerable Kids are out of touch with their feelings. They often say, "I don't know."

Frequently, when asked, Vulnerable Kids will say that they don't "feel." They really don't. They talk and act as though they were numb. They are. These children hold on to grudges and don't express feelings because they are concerned with what will happen if they get angry or antagonistic. These children cannot afford to feel because they don't have the confidence to handle their feelings and don't have the adult support they need to share their feelings. There is no one, in their view, to comfort them when they are sad, to accept them when they are angry, to share in their joy, to reassure them when they are disappointed, or to direct them when they are confused. They live inside an emotional vacuum, afraid of being rejected by the adults around them because they have or express these feelings. It becomes easier and less threatening for them to keep the feelings inside and deny that they even have them than to acknowledge them. Eventually, through lack of practice, they lose the ability, even for themselves, to distinguish how and what they are feeling.

When life smacks *them* in the face, even sometimes in minor ways, they don't get hurt, they get damaged.

Capable Kids can bend. Vulnerable Kids can break.

How to Know What You Are Feeling

It takes practice to know what you are feeling. The world seems to be organized to distract you from knowing. Infants know, and they let the people around them know, too. But as children grow, many influences work on them to mute the signals that are given off by their own bodies to their own brains.

Knowing what you are feeling involves getting re-acquainted with your body and the signals it gives. It also involves becoming familiar with the typical pattern of thoughts that go along with specific feelings for you.

To help your child to return to an awareness of his own feelings, look over the following list. Sit down with your child and talk it through. Describe your memories of times when you experienced these feelings yourself. You will have made giant strides if all you do is enable both of you to become comfortable with these words. The words lead to the concepts and the concepts lead to the feelings.

Any child who can comfortably talk and feel his way through this list is ready for whatever stress life throws at him.

calm	guilty	frightened
warm	safe	confident
excited	strong	interested
willing	happy	competitive
contented	busy	angry
joyous	loving	frustrated
grouchy	lonely	sorry
sad	dumb	rebellious
anxious	put down	confused
tired	silly	restless
nervous	shy	bored
ashamed	hurt	

Focus on the Big Five

Of all the feelings that circulate through your child's body and mind, there are five that are basic. Let's look at them one by one. They are

love
joy
frustration
fear
anger

Love

Capable Kids know that they are loved and that they love. They are comfortable with words that express love and can freely say "I love you."

Capable Kids like to hug and kiss and to be hugged and kissed. They feel relaxed about the physical contact involved in the straightforward kind of hugs and kisses, the kind that demonstrate love.

Capable Kids are sensitive to, and shy away from, manipulative hugs and kisses that represent control rather than genuine affection. Capable Kids do not appear hungry for hugs and kisses; rather, they appear comfortable with them. Capable Kids do not *demand* physical affection, they enjoy it.

Vulnerable Kids are reticent about love. They are reluctant to say "I love you." The words have to be dragged out of them if they are to be heard.

Vulnerable Kids are stiff and uncomfortable when hugged. They duck away from kisses. They do not volunteer kisses and hugs to other people, even those they want to love. Vulnerable children are self-conscious about getting and giving love.

Betsy is eleven and a half. Her mother told me that one

day Betsy looked at her mother and said, "You know, Mom, you look low. Maybe you need some extra hugs and kisses." Betsy is a Capable Kid.

Susan is also eleven. She is a client of mine whom I have seen for two years. Her parents are divorced, and her mother has been hospitalized for "nervous break-downs" on and off since Susan was six years old. Although Susan is getting somewhat better, she still has never asked me anything about myself, not even a routine "How are you?" She is so cut off from her feelings, so suspicious of love, that she thinks that if she doesn't ask, she won't know, and she won't have to deal with anything that might make an emotional demand on her. She is terrified of having to feel and has a difficult time being touched. She seems to shrink into herself when someone tries to offer her physical closeness. Susan is a Vulnerable Kid.

Joy

Capable Kids, when they are elated, *show* that they are elated. A Capable Kid who receives a gift that he very much wants is wreathed in smiles and laughter. He jumps with excitement. He hugs and kisses and bounces around. When he scores a good grade on a test or is invited to a party or makes a basket in a game, he appears happy.

Capable Kids are usually happy, because they are not afraid of their own feelings of anger and sadness. They accept those feelings and know that, if circumstances bring them such feelings, they will know how to deal with them. This frees them to express joy, glee, and happiness when something good occurs in their lives.

Vulnerable Kids do *not* express glee. They do not "jump for joy." They are too worried that something bad will happen. In fact, what Vulnerable Kids deal with is a whole collection of the bad things that have already happened, as bad things routinely happen in anyone's life. Instead of letting these things go, they pile all the bad things one on top of another until they are carrying around their entire past negative history.

Vulnerable Kids find it almost impossible to feel, much less express, unbridled joy. They cannot easily smile or give off an air of excitement because they have so many other feelings in the way, feelings that are not being owned up to or dealt with. Vulnerable Kids do not express joy, because they are too busy lying to themselves. They are preoccupied with telling themselves that they do *not* feel what, indeed, they *do* feel. And what they do feel is *not* joy but fear and anger.

Chris is twelve. He wanted a stereo for his birthday, and when he opened the package and found one, he ran to his mom and hugged and kissed her, then threw his arms around his dad's neck and thanked him profusely. Next he ran to the phone, called his best friend, and babbled the news, then came back to finish unpacking, saying "I can't believe it. This is so exciting. Thanks so much. You guys are so generous." He went immediately to his room with his treasure and started setting up the speakers. Chris is a Capable Kid.

David, ten, auditioned for the lead in the class play. When the teacher called home that night to announce that he had won the part, only the flicker of a smile crossed his face. He displayed very little energy. After he hung up, his mother said, "Aren't you pleased?" David then proceeded to list a dozen reasons why it wouldn't be a good thing. "I'll probably louse it up," he said. "I can't remember all those lines. I'll look stupid in the costume." Discouraged by the prospect of the hard work involved, David dropped out of the play.

David is a Vulnerable Kid.

Frustration

All children experience frustration. Watch a baby trying to learn to walk. He pulls himself up, starts out, falls down, goes back at it, falls again, then tries once more. There's frustration in that process, of course, but he does not let it stop him. He climbs back up each time and keeps going.

Capable Kids maintain that attitude toward frustration long after their baby days are over. They do not let frustration bog them down.

Capable Kids use their frustration in a form that challenges them. They turn it into motivation.

Vulnerable Kids let frustration stop them or turn them aside. When Vulnerable Kids experience frustration, they quit.

John is a Capable Kid and Paul is a Vulnerable Kid. They are working together on a model train. They fuss over the cars and tracks for hours. When they have everything set up just the way they want it, they flip the switch, but the train doesn't start.

Paul gets angry and stomps off to his room, muttering, "It's a dumb train, anyway. Who cares."

John gets angry, too, but minutes later he is bending over the train, trying to figure out what is wrong.

Fear

All children also experience fear. Capable children are not ruled by it; vulnerable children are.

Capable Kids are willing to take risks. They do not avoid people, circumstances, or events because they are afraid. They overcome their fear and go ahead with what they want to do.

Their risks are basically sensible ones, because they are aware of danger. They do not do "crazy" things, but they do enjoy a sense of adventure.

Vulnerable Kids feel fear *most* of the time. Fear is both their motivation and their limitation.

Vulnerable Kids have difficulty moving ahead into what appears to them uncharted territory. They view risk taking as much too scary. Instead, because they do not value their own lives as healthy children do, they may involve themselves in potentially self-destructive activities. Vulnerable Kids are the ones who race cars while they are drinking or fall into dangerous drug usage.

Frankie is five and he wants to go down the big slide at the amusement park. He is afraid, but he sees the other kids laughing and he wants to try it. He makes his uncle promise to keep an arm around him until they get going. Gritting his teeth, he climbs the ladder to get on the slide. On the slide, once he starts picking up speed, he relaxes and screams with joy all the way to the bottom. He pleads to go on again. Frankie is a Capable Kid.

Mark, seven, is constantly complaining. He repeatedly says to his mother, "Mom, I can't. I'm afraid." For whatever she wants him to do, he has an excuse why he can't do it. Usually it is because he doesn't know how or won't be good at it. Yet one day, while he is with his friends, he climbs to the top of a silo near where he lives and, literally risking his life, walks, like a tightrope walker, all the way around the edge. He swears his playmates to secrecy because he knows his mother would be hysterical if she knew what he had done. Still, when she is out of earshot, he brags about his stunt. Mark is a Vulnerable Kid.

Anger

Of all the basic feelings that spell the difference between Capable Kids and Vulnerable Kids, anger is, in my opinion, the most significant. It is the emotion most confused and misused in our society.

Anger blocks all other feelings. A child who does not own his anger, who does not accept it, experience it, and let it go, cannot feel anything. A child who is bottling up his anger is preoccupied, inside himself, with that anger. It is, quite simply, in his way. As long as he is carrying it around, he cannot see, hear, or experience anything else with any degree of depth. No matter what happens in his life, when he opens up, even a crack, it is anger that boils out. He is the most vulnerable of the Vulnerable Kids.

A Capable Kid experiences his anger. He allows himself to feel it, then he lets it go. If he can learn something from the experience that caused the anger, so much the better.

The Vulnerable Kid holds on to his anger, explodes or not, depending on the situation, then turns the anger inward, where it festers into discouragement and depression. He may project his anger onto someone else, hurling blame at whomever he can, but he almost always reserves a major portion of the blame for himself. He may not blame himself *out loud*. That is usually something he does to himself, by himself.

The Vulnerable Kid, passively sitting on his volcano of anger, sees himself as helpless. He is the consummate victim. There is nothing, in his view, that he can do to change the situation, whatever it may be. He can only cover it over, at least for the present. He waits to "read" the situation or "get the drift" of events, but he does not shape them.

The Vulnerable Kid stays with his anger. It is familiar to him. He is often the child with the "short fuse" who is so difficult to have around, the one who is always ready for a battle, who always has his "dukes up." He is the child who pops off, spilling torrents of anger, at the slightest provocation.

He can also be the child who keeps it all bottled up inside, complaining constantly about something or other, finding fault with the nicest people, tearing apart the pleasantest experience. He is the child who sees only the bugs at the picnic, hears only the sour notes at the concert, remembers only the slighting remark, never the compliment.

Tim gets back a social-studies test and finds that even

though he studied, he got a bad grade. He tells his mother about it. "I'm furious," he says. "Damn. I needed that grade, too. I'll have to hit it really hard next time." He thinks about it for a while, then drops it to concentrate on something else. The next time there's a test, he arranges to study with a friend who is doing better than he is in social studies. Going into the test, he feels more confident, and he pulls a better grade. Tim is a Capable Kid.

Linda is extemely angry with her father, who is dying of cancer. He has been a neglectful father and, now that he is sick, she just sits and stares at him when he complains of his pain. She does not ask him how he feels or demonstrate any other concern for him. She hasn't told him about her anger, and now that he is dying, it is greater than ever. She knows he won't have a chance to make it up to her and be the loving father she wants. Linda has turned her anger inward and is depressed and grossly overweight. She has few friends. Linda is a Vulnerable Kid.

Why Kids Are What They Are

The Capable Kid knows how he feels and knows *why* he feels the way he does.

He will carry that knowledge and the ability to do something about his feelings with him throughout his life.

The Vulnerable Kid does not know what he feels. He does not know why he has such difficulty feeling feelings. He does not know what to do about it.

We, you and I, and all the adults in his life, must help him. Not feeling is really too much pain to carry through a lifetime.

Exercise

GUESS WHAT I'M FEELING

Any number of family members can play this game, as long as all agree to take it seriously. That doesn't mean you can't laugh. You can, and I hope you will. It means that no one in the game will be making fun of it or of the people playing. Malicious teasing arouses feelings that will get in the way of identifying any other feelings you will want to be aware of and deal with. It's also a good game for one parent, alone, to play with one child. Whether or not the two of you comprise the family, feelings may be expressed between the two of you that either might be reluctant to display to others.

Turn back to page 170 for the list of frequently experienced feelings.

Write each feeling on a separate index card. Shuffle the cards. Ask everyone in the game to pick one. Have each player in turn pantomime the feeling. Have everyone else guess what the feeling is.

If the children are young or for some other reason are having a particularly hard time identifying feelings, talk about clues you pick up from their facial expressions or bodily postures. Examples are "Your mouth looked sad" or "I could tell from the way your shoulders slumped that you were tired" or "You were jumping up and down as if you were very happy." They'll get the idea.

Next, have each player tell about an experience he had in which he felt that emotion. For example: "I was teased at school when I got braces and I got angry." "Yesterday when my sister wouldn't listen to me, I felt frustrated." "It makes me feel happy and loved when you bring me home a flower." Keep to simple, common experiences and reactions to them. You can inject more complex situations and emotions, if you want, as the game progresses. Just be careful not to leave your child behind. Concentrate on the feelings and keep them connected with the events and circumstances that cause them.

Exercise

VENTING FEELINGS

Ask your child to choose two feelings that he has particular trouble expressing and have him state why. Because this can be difficult for anyone, especially a child, it is a good idea for you to go first. Be honest. Choose two feelings that you *do* have trouble expressing and state why. You may surprise yourself by learning that when you say these things out loud, they automatically become a little easier to face. For example: "I have trouble with anger. I usually know when I'm angry, but I tell myself I'm not so that I won't have to do anything about it."

You can get more specific if you want to and if you feel comfortable doing so. Your child, you may find, will be interested in your "confessions" but quite anxious to get on with spilling his own bottled-up feelings. For instance, he may also choose anger. (This is a popular choice. As you know from your own experiences and from accounts of violence in the daily press, more people have trouble with the healthy expression of anger than with most other emotions.)

Your child may surprise you with a statement such as "If I get angry at Grandma, I'm afraid she won't think I'm a good girl and won't take care of me anymore, and then you won't be able to work and we won't have any money."

If your child can admit to this kind of feeling, consider yourself, and the game, a major success. You now have an opportunity to deal with those feelings and fears and help him work out a way to handle them.

Your child may make a statement such as "I'm not good about love. If I tell Dad I love him, he will ignore me and then I'll feel dumb."

This gives you an opportunity to help him work out a way to reach his goal. Ask him if he wants help figuring out a way to tell his father that he loves him. Don't impose your desires and feelings onto your child. This is a game for him. There may be problems between you and his father that cannot and should not enter into this exchange. But all of you can only profit from an honest ability to feel your feelings.

Like other exercises in this book, this one may seem silly and awkward at first, but don't give up, and don't be discouraged.

Children, even the ones who seem squirmy and embarrassed, appreciate your interest and concern in helping them feel better about themselves.

PART 3

Stress-Proofing

12
Reconnecting the Mind-Body Connection

Do you want additional proof of the importance to your child of the material and the exercises in this book? That is the purpose of this chapter. I would like to take you briefly into the professional literature and research that has been done on the connection between the mind and the body. I hope to convince you, beyond a shadow of a doubt, that what you do now, how you teach, train, and model for your child, will profoundly affect his well-being, his health, and happiness for the rest of his life.

What this chapter is about, what the research detailed here shows, has very little to do with actual illness. It has everything to do with your and, therefore, your child's attitudes toward illness and wellness. How you raise your children, I believe, has as much or more to do with their ultimate health and well-being than the genes you pass on to them. And the research has proven it.

Earlier in this book, I talked about the importance of validating our children so that they can handle stress. If they can handle stress, they can conquer almost anything. And if they have the feeling that they can conquer, they can learn to be healthy.

Dr. Carolyn B. Thomas, a professor at Johns Hopkins University School of Medicine and the head of its Precursor Study, began a research project in 1946 looking for early clues to disease. She was particularly interested in diseases of the heart. She selected 1,337 medical students, carefully detailed their medical, genetic, and psychological histories, and studied them for years. She gave particular attention, in yearly questionnaires and interviews, to her subjects' attitudes and personality characteristics. She analyzed their childhoods, family lives, goals, emotional outlooks, and even details about such personal habits as smoking, drinking, and coffee consumption.

As these doctors progressed through their lives into their mid-fifties and sixties, there was, of course, an increase in the incidence of disease and death among them. But in addition to documenting the obvious, Dr. Thomas turned up some interesting and unexpected findings.

She found that there was a difference between the doctors who remained healthy and those who became sick. She found two distinct patterns. There were "the winners," who maintained their robustness throughout their life-spans, and "the losers," who sickened and died early.

After studying this phenomenon and isolating the factor that made the difference between the two groups, she gave it a name. She called it "stamina."

Stamina, Dr. Thomas concluded, was the strength to withstand disease, fatigue, or hardship. She found that the stamina factor contained two additional components, which she called "resistance" and "stability." Dr. Thomas concluded that stamina was a condition of harmony between the mind and the body. She attributed it to the combination of our genes, our attitudes, and our upbringing.

Of course the key questions, once this factor had been isolated, were What makes up this condition called stamina? and What creates it?

Dr. Thomas found four important components. The person with stamina, she learned, has

1. an openness and flexibility in his approach to life
2. a spontaneous, outgoing temperament
3. high self-esteem
4. a minimum of tension, anxiety, and anger while under stress.

An offshoot of Dr. Thomas's work, the Hopkins study, focused on victims of suicide attempts, mental illness, and cancer. Those studied reported feeling a lack of closeness to a parent or parents when they were children. They remember experiencing their fathers as cold rather than warm, unloving rather than loving, or their mothers as detached.

By contrast, the healthy subjects in this study remembered experiencing their parents as warm and understanding. Men's relationships with their fathers were usually described as comfortable. The relationships between their parents were seen by subjects as congenial and relaxed.

These healthy subjects, while under stress, often reported feeling some of the same reactions as those reported by the mental illness and suicide-attempt victims. What the study disclosed, however, was that they felt *fewer* reactions and for a shorter period of time.

In other words, healthy people experience the same stress reactions, the same anxiety, and physical symptoms, but they are able to let go of them sooner and move on to more positive phases of their lives.

Study after study shows that our attitudes and feelings have a tremendous influence and effect on our bodies' state of wellness or illness, that our minds and bodies work together, not independently of each other. The studies prove, too, that those most vulnerable to life's stresses and to premature disease may be compromised at any point, throughout their lifetimes, by chronic subconscious stresses and emotions that orginate in childhood.

Studies have shown that passive emotional states, such as grief and hopelessness, trigger responses in the brain. Long-term unconscious stresses, in particular, can cause chronic secretion of cortisol. Scientists are beginning to learn that this substance can undermine the immune system's ability to resist arthritis, cancer, or infectious diseases.

Nonpassive, aggressive emotions, such as anger and impatience, release hormones and chemicals known as catecholamines, including adrenaline. While adrenaline, which greatly increases strength, can be vital for survival, its prolonged or frequent release can bring on high blood pressure, which can lead to headaches, kidney problems, strokes, or heart attacks.

The body is consistently seeking a condition of homeostasis, its own equilibrium. Under stress, it attempts to compensate for the disruption by activating its own biochemical adaptations or changes. The price we pay for this physical imbalance can be a greater vulnerability to disease.

Sidney Cobb, a physician who is former president of the American Psychosomatic Society, has observed the mind-body connection closely. He has said, "There is a great need for a family environment that allows us to be ourselves and to express ourselves openly, by accepting children for who and what they are and forgetting trying to create that 'perfect child.'" Dr. Cobb emphasizes the vital role played in human development by physical contact between parents and their children. "Body contact," he states, "is very important. Especially hugs."

As a result of his observations and research, he has concluded that warm, loving relationships are vital for the development of self-esteem.

How Personality Profiles Correlate to Illness

Back in the 1950s and 1960s, researchers began turning up strong indications that there were connections between certain personality traits and susceptibility to cancer. Serious studies linking these factors were published in 1952, 1954, 1956, 1957, 1958, 1961, and 1967. A summary of these studies shows that the person who is cancer-prone tends to have had an unhappy childhood that included either loss from divorce or disease, or a feeling of estrangement because parents frequently fought. As a result of these conditions, these people developed into lonely, anxious, helpless, self-hating adults. In order to achieve the love they felt they had missed as children, these studies concluded, these individuals tended to try too hard to please others. Typically, these people, upon getting some positive feedback from the world, such as success in a job or love from a mate or a child, tended to make the source of that feedback all important. Then, if the circuit was broken, if the job or business success was lost or the loved one died or rejected them, these cancer-prone personalities were found to relapse, over time, into the anxious, lonely, hopeless, self-hating children they once had been. It appeared as if despair and bitterness, locked up inside them, unexpressed, was transformed into or made them susceptible to cancer, which began to eat away at them.

This research is reported in *Getting Well Again* by

Stephanie Simonton, whose work was discussed in chapters 1, 6, and 8.

Another study suggests that the foundation for heart disease too can lie in childhood. This study was conducted by Gerald Berenson and others at Louisiana State University, and it demonstrated that the same Type A behavior linked to heart-attack–prone personalities in adults shows up in children in the form of a higher-than-normal level of cholesterol in the bloodstream.

Type A behavior, in adults or in children, is characterized by restlessness, hostility, tension, and an over-developed sense of time urgency.

The LSU study examined 378 children aged ten to seventeen in Franklinton, Louisiana, and was the outgrowth of a larger study in nearby Bogalusa. As a result of his study, Dr. Berenson expressed the hope that eventually doctors would be able to use its findings to treat children's heart risks before they grew into life-threatening adult dangers.

Psychosomatic Illness in Children

Many children routinely respond to frustration in their lives with symptoms that imitate, or that are, those of physical illnesses. What mother of a school-aged child has not heard the whiny complaints of a "Monday-morning stomachache." School social workers can tell vivid stories of stomachaches, headaches, or worse that have developed in children as they attempted to deal with problems in their homes. Nurses and doctors have all seen children, referred by other doctors or clinic staffs, with baffling, unexplained, and inexplicable symptoms.

Usually what happens is this: a parent brings a child into a doctor's office, clinic, or hospital because she feels there is some organic problem causing the symptoms. When no organic cause can be found, a social worker or psychologist is brought in and asked to help in making a diagnosis or offering treatment. Psychosomatic illnesses in children often include asthma, ulcers, stomachaches, headaches, and pains in the arms and legs.

Many experts have offered theories about what causes psychosomatic illness and why some children develop it and others do not. Jane Kessler, in *Psychopathology of Childhood*, suggests that certain personality traits give rise to certain psychosomatic illnesses.

Harold and Helen Kaplan, in the *American Journal of Psychiatry*, June 1959, suggest that chronic tension may produce a variety of psychosomatic illnesses in constitutionally susceptible individuals if their psychological defenses are inadequate to reduce their anxious or excited states.

An example of the complex psychological and physiological factors involved in this process can be seen by observing the suffering of children who have asthma. The unconscious meaning of this illness has often been described as suppressed crying. To a child who suffers from asthma, however, there is nothing imaginary about the attacks and the medical procedures that follow them. They can be terrifying and painful. There are people who remain hampered in their ability to function in adult life by memories of asthmatic attacks in childhood, moments when they felt helpless and overwhelmed, unable to breathe.

It is impossible to discuss the treatment of psychosomatic illness in children without considering the families in which the children live. Research studies such as Jane Kessler's have disclosed much that is valuable in this area as well. Mothers whose children develop such ailments tend to appear to their children as cold and manipulative. They tend to be the kinds of mothers who convey approval to their children for what they do, rather than for what they are. These mothers are sometimes found to mask their unconscious hostility with overprotection of their children. They often suffer themselves from psychosomatic symptoms.

Fathers in such families are frequently perceived as passive or detached. These homes are often described as tense with unexpressed conflicts. The children of these families often appear to others to be "too good."

A Personal Glimpse

I hope this brief dip into the vast library of research studies convinces you of the mind-body connection.

Now, in a more personal way, I'd like to show you how this all works by introducing you to a little girl I knew.

Her name is Bonita. She was only six years old when she lost her parents. Sent away from home and everything familiar to live with an aunt and uncle she hardly knew, in a place she had never been before, she developed a stiff neck. It lasted for an entire year!

The aunt and uncle dragged her to doctor after doctor, but no one could find a physical reason for her pain. She was teased and taunted, accused of malingering and faking. It was awful. It amazes me that anyone would not realize that a child that young suffering that much pain for such a long time had something serious going on inside of her somewhere.

I remember that incident as if it were yesterday. It was as if the little girl didn't want to turn her head to see what was around her or behind her. She was scared stiff!

Bonita is my sister.

Exercise

THE BEST PREVENTION

Take your child by the hand. Go out for a walk. Move fast enough to feel your muscles working. Slow down enough to notice the insects, the flowers, the cracks in the sidewalk, and the neighbors along the way.

Come home.

Hug each other.

13

You Feel as Well as You Eat

My mom took most of the sugar out of the house last year and I was really mad at her at first. I'm used to having licorice and other stuff in the cookie jar. Finally, I started thinking about it. Then I got really sick from the change. Then I started feeling a lot better. Finally, I came to my senses. Now I think it was really smart of my mother to take the sugar out of the house. It's like so-o-o tempting when I go to parties. At my friend's party, she had a humungous cake and it looked so good, and I took a little piece with a lot of frosting and I felt really sick afterwards. I wanted to barf! Once you go off sugar you have to stay off. It's really bad for you. Now, I'm getting better from the torture that I gave to my body when I was eating sugar. I feel good and I can really taste food now.

—Becky Cutler, age 9

Sometimes people associate good nutrition with eating health food and stuff like that. That's not true. One day my mom emptied out every little grain of sugar. I came home from school and there wasn't anything there. No pure sugar, no powdered sugar for cooking, no cookies, no candy, no chocolate syrup, no ice cream. The hardest part was no cookies.

It took us a long time to adjust. You get sugar withdrawal and everything. I got headaches and felt really tired. Then your body stops depending on sugar. Then you start seeing what has been happening to you. My knees are bad, and when I eat sugar it affects my knees. With different people it's different things. I see things now that are really gross. I know a kid who comes to school with two pieces of white bread, which isn't good for you in the first place because of bleached flour, and between them he has a layer of chocolate!

I find now that I can handle the stress of my life, like a pop quiz or something, much better than the kids who eat like that and spend their allowances on candy bars.

—Brett Cutler, age 14

Bookstores and magazine racks are packed with guidelines to good nutrition, and most of us know the basics of healthy eating. I'd like to focus here on some villains, the hidden "bad guys" that have slipped into our children's diets and are not only bad for their physical health but powerful enough to ruin the beneficial effects of our best efforts at stress education.

The Relationship Between Stress and Nutrition

As a source of stress, a poor diet is second only to emotional pressures. Given our modern dietary habits, we are almost constantly threatening ourselves with serious chemical and nutritional imbalances.

Experts in the field of nutrition tell us over and over that the American diet is a national disaster. We pay far too little attention to the quality of the food we eat. We don't even know how to eat our food properly. We eat too fast. We don't chew well. We eat too much. Despite the number of cookbooks and kitchen gadgets, millions of us have lost the art of cooking and preparing good food. We allow junk food, in one form or other, to dominate our diets. And all this has a price—constant stress.

It's a problem that is simple to understand and relatively easy to fix. Two complementary dietary processes go on in the human body. One is nourishing. The other is cleansing. If we don't regulate them with the proper dietary habits, the body gradually builds up toxins that form the basis for many mental and physical difficulties.

Fresh, nutritious, and simple are the food qualities that are best for our health. But amazingly, sixty to seventy percent of the American diet is below optimal nutritional value. This is not because we do not have enough food to eat, but because so much of what we eat is not useful to us.

Five Nutritional Enemies

It is essential that we regulate our diets to keep our bodies from creating stress. In my opinion, there are five principle villains in our modern diet. They are sugar, caffeine, salt, chemical additives, and junk food. By learning to recognize and avoid them and by teaching your children to do the same, you will have moved a major step forward in your journey toward conquering stress.

Sugar

Refined sugar, which has absolutely no nutritional value, makes up twenty-five percent of our diet. (You should also know that fats, which likewise have no nutrients, make up forty-five percent. That's a total of seventy percent of our food. No wonder that we and our children have a hard time dealing with stress. We are operating on low levels of fuel!)

Besides dramatically increasing our nutrient debt, refined sugar leads to conditions that are directly bad for our health, among them obesity, a major disease of modern society. Also, the precipitous rise and decline of blood sugar caused by the intake of refined sugar can lead to a strain on the liver as well as imbalances in insulin production. This in turn can lead to both hypoglycemia and diabetes. Either of these conditions can pose serious threats to the nervous system. Low blood sugar, or hypoglycemia, has also been associated with psychological stress. People who have it complain of and manifest anxiety, restlessness, tiredness, and depression. Diabetes is even more serious. It can lead to impaired circulation, heart and kidney damage, deafness, or blindness. Indeed, a diabetic coma can kill.

While sugar in the blood is a major fuel for our cells, we don't need to supply it artificially. We get naturally occurring sugar in a well-balanced diet that contains fresh fruits, vegetables, and grains.

It is important to be aware of the sugar content of our food, because sugar is a stimulant and leads to heightened arousal. Refined sugar is too much of a stimulant for the body to handle comfortably.

So you can know it when you see it, the other names for sugar are

sucrose
corn syrup

lactose
turbinado sugar
dextrose
invert sugar
fructose
maltose
honey
glucose
molasses
maple sugar and syrup

The symptoms of too much sugar intake can include

mental health problems
dental cavities
obesity
hypoglycemia (too little sugar in the blood), characterized by fatigue, nervousness, irritability,
depression, weakness, faintness, dizziness,
headaches, heart palpitations, inability to concentrate
diabetes
heart disease
susceptibility to disease
skin problems
splitting nails
lifeless hair

Foods with high sugar content that should be avoided
are

candy
cakes
cookies
sweetened cereal
powdered and canned drinks
puddings

ice cream
gum
mints

Caffeine

In research conducted at the University of Michigan, psychiatrist John F. Greden determined, through a wide range of tests administered to one hundred volunteers, that a condition called caffeinism does exist. Heavy caffeine consumers, those who drink eight to ten cups of coffee or cola a day, were compared to light caffeine consumers and were found, in high proportions, to be severely depressed. The heavy caffeine users displayed symptoms such as

headaches
dizziness
frequent urination
free-floating anxiety

Other researchers have linked these symptoms to caffeine use:

abnormally fast heartbeat
abnormal heart rhythms or extra heartbeats
increased blood pressure
digestive disorders
heartburn
fevers
breast lumps

Foods high in caffeine are

brewed coffee
instant coffee
coffee-grain blends

leaf tea
instant tea
colas
Dr. Pepper
cocoa
chocolate

Salt

The minimum daily requirement for human consumption of salt is extremely low. Patients on therapeutic diets for various conditions have seen their health improve dramatically when their intake of salt is kept to 150 mg., or less than one-eighth teaspoon per day. In contrast, the average American eats from 5,000 to 10,000 mg. of salt, between one and two teaspoons, per day. Large quantities of processed or snack food can raise this total to more than four teaspoons.

Although salt has been highly prized throughout history for its taste, nutritionists have been unable to find a need for it in the human diet. Animals, including man, can develop a salt habit; many animals have been shown to walk long distances to find a "salt lick."

Recent research has disclosed links between salt intake and the incidence of high blood pressure and other conditions that seriously affect the heart and its functioning. Beyond that, the overuse of salt can have a deleterious effect on the body's ability to absorb potassium, which is a nutritionally essential element of the diet.

The symptoms of the overuse of salt include

hypertension
obesity
heart and kidney disease
migraine headaches
seizures

nervous tension
swelling and puffiness of face and ankles

Foods heavy in salt content are

processed cereals
packaged breads
canned soups
luncheon meats
frozen and canned vegetables
fast foods
packaged desserts
packaged mixes

After sugar, salt is the leading food additive in America, both in factory-prepared food and in home cooking. There is some naturally occurring salt in fresh foods, meat, and vegetables, and in water. But a startling two-thirds of the salt in our diet comes from processed convenience foods.

Here are some suggestions for ways to cut down on salt usage:

Take the salt shaker off the dining table.
Gradually reduce the amount of salt used in cooking and baking.
Experiment with herbs and spices in place of salt.
Reduce consumption of convenience foods.
When using canned vegetables, drain liquid and rinse contents with water.
Read labels for salt content.
Check salt level in tap water.
Avoid softened water.

Chemical Additives

Each year, every American consumes an estimated five pounds of chemicals that do not occur naturally in the food chain. That's a lot of material to put into your body that nature didn't intend to be there.

There are over two thousand additives commonly used by the food industry. The effect on us of this barrage of chemicals is still not known, but when you add to them the herbicides and pesticides in and on the food that we swallow, we know they are not doing us any good. Indeed, there is an almost constant public controversy over the safety of one additive or another. Many have already been removed from the market as health hazards. We still do not know the long-term effects of these chemical mixtures on the delicately balanced mechanisms that are our bodies.

Since World War II, the consumption of soft drinks in this country has increased by eighty percent, pastries by seventy percent, and potato chips by eighty-five percent. On the other hand, the consumption of dairy products has decreased by twenty-one percent, vegetables by twenty-three percent, and fruits by twenty-five percent.

Studies have linked food-coloring additives to hyperactivity in children, and internal-organ damage and cancer in animals.

DES, a chemical used to fatten animals, has been proven to be cancer-producing, and its use has been banned since 1979.

Nitrates and nitrites, found in bacon, hot dogs, ham, luncheon meat, knockwurst, processed meats, and drinking water contaminated by fertilizer from farmlands have been found to be cancer-producing.

Additives to avoid include

> artificial coloring agents blue #1 and #2, citrus red #2, green #3, red #3 and #40, yellow #5.
> BVO (brominated vegetable oil)
> MSG (monosodium glutamate)
> quinine

saccharine
sodium nitrates and nitrites

Foods that contain an overabundance of chemicals*
include

packaged candy
cold cuts
sausages
packaged cakes
many brands of ice cream
prepared frozen foods
frozen ice treats
powdered beverage mixes
packaged instant foods
packaged side dishes
overprocessed white bread
artificial potato chips
prepared artificial juices
processed cheese spreads

Here are some suggestions for keeping your additive
consumption under reasonable control:

Eat a wide variety of foods.
Use fresh and/or minimally processed foods.
Use real foods, not imitations.
Read labels.

Hyperactivity and Chemicals: In the past few years, a
tremendous amount of research has been conducted that
links hyperactivity in children with chemical additives.
This can be good news about a serious worry for many

---

*Some foods labeled "No Preservatives" are heavily treated with
other chemicals.

parents. If you have a hyperactive child, you probably do
not need this book to point it out to you. Your state of
exhaustion has already made it clear. But here are some of
the symptoms of a hyperactive child:

> He pays attention to everything around him and is
> unable to screen out distractions in order to
> concentrate on the task in front of him.
> He is jumpy, in constant motion, "can't sit still." He
> touches anything he can reach.
> He has a short attention span, frequently dropping
> what he is doing, leaving it unfinished, to move
> on to something else.
> He is forgetful.
> He may also be aggressive, hostile, irritable, or
> overly emotional.
> He dismantles or destroys his toys, your possessions,
> books, magazines, or anything left within his
> reach.
> He has a low threshold for pain. He bursts easily into
> tears or giggles.
> He is demanding, insisting on having things "my
> way."
> He is disruptive and talkative during class.
> He teases other children.
> He is clumsy, impatient, and often loses his pos-
> sessions.
> He has nervous habits such as sucking on his blanket
> or clothes, biting or picking his fingernails,
> twirling, sucking, or pulling his hair.
> He is accident-prone. He attempts reckless stunts
> that hurt him.
> He talks loudly, excessively, or rapidly and inter-
> rupts others.
> He panics easily.
> As a baby, he appeared colicky, sucked his thumb or

pacifier intensely, rocked his crib, or banged his head when angry.

Numerous studies of children with behavior problems have yielded some dramatic findings. Many such children have chemical imbalances; food allergies; hypoglycemia; reactions to food additives, coloring agents, or preservatives; or addictions to junk food or sugar.

Hyperactivity in children is sometimes treated in ways that do not help. Sometimes it is not treated at all. Some doctors prescribe stimulants, such as a type of amphetamine that slows impulses to the brain. Other doctors oppose the use of drugs, which can produce side effects.

Dr. Ben Feingold's extremely valuable book *Why Your Child Is Hyperactive* describes a specific diet for the hyperactive child. Dr. Feingold reports that his work began with allergic patients who were also hyperactive. He found that in clearing up the complaints associated with allergic reactions, the hyperactive behavior also diminished. Gradually Dr. Feingold turned his attention to synthetic food additives. He developed a diet that excludes all foods and drugs that contain artificial coloring or flavoring. Results reported by parents who have put their hyperactive children on this diet have ranged from a moderate improvement to dramatic improvement. There are people who claim that the Feingold diet has turned their children from jumpy, crazy nonachievers into successful, happy kids.

Junk Food

The main ingredients of junk or snack food are sugar, refined flour, salt, and chemical additives used to enhance flavor and color and to extend shelf life. For all the reasons previously discussed about the effects of these ingredients on the system, there can be little doubt that taking in vast quantities of them can adversely affect a child's physical well-being, emotional equilibrium, and therefore his level of stress.

Convenience or processed foods, which have become increasingly popular since World War II, are notoriously lacking in nutritional value and fiber, which has become recognized as a dietary necessity. Most processed food, and junk food in particular, is intentionally designed to appeal to our primary taste sensations, those of sweetness, saltiness, and sourness. They contain heavy quantitites of sugar or salt, so that eating them rapidly leaves a sweet or salty taste in the mouth. Their real appearance, odor, and flavor are disguised by a variety of chemicals. The words *enhanced* or *imitation* on the label are clues that what is inside that package is largely or wholly chemicals, not food.

What can you do to keep junk food out of your kids? You are up against its easy availability, its cheapness, and the peer pressure to eat it. One thing you can do is to have alternatives available—fruit (fresh or dried), unsalted nuts, peanut butter, unsalted popcorn, and natural fruit drinks. When children come home from school or are hungry at night, you can make sure that there is food around that is good for them, that tastes good, and that *is* good.

There is not much you can do about what your children eat when they are away from you. But certainly you can influence them by what you have for them at home. By not having junk food in the house, by cleaning out soda pop, potato chips, corn chips, candies, cakes, and cookies, you will give them the opportunity to become used to eating the kinds of foods that are much better for them.

Attitudes Toward Food

It is parents who adversely influence their children to grow into the people who use food as stress relief, who make food the center of their lives.

Here are some suggestions from parents on running a household in which kids learn instead the principles of good nutrition:

Keep nourishing nibble food, such as popcorn, nuts, seeds, fruits, and vegetables around and available.

Serve fresh fruit for dessert, and/or cut down drastically on sugar when making desserts.

Change from white bread to whole wheat bread.

Eliminate soft drinks. Substitute fruit juices.

Read labels in the supermarket to make sure that you are purchasing foods with as few additives and fats and as little sugar and sodium as possible.

Cook carefully. Do not overcook or fry food.

Institute changes slowly, one at a time.

Don't use sweets and desserts as rewards.

Don't tell your family that something is "good" for them. This can be an instant turnoff.

Try to make the dinner table a pleasant place rather than a battleground.

Don't make an issue out of nutrition, so that it becomes a power struggle between you and your child over what he is or is not going to eat.

Get the children involved in good nutrition. Take them grocery shopping with you. Involve them in meal planning and cooking.

Focus on what they are eating at home. Don't try to "police" what they eat when you are not with them.

Keep a list of good nutritious foods on the bulletin board or refrigerator so that your child is con-

stantly being educated on the subject without
your preaching to him.

Here, in the words of the mother whose children you
heard from at the beginning of this chapter, is how she
managed a nutrition transition in her family:

> I took all the sugar out of our house one day. I've
> never been one to do things gradually. But if I had it
> to do over, I wouldn't have been so abrupt. My fam-
> ily balked, to put it mildly. My husband threatened
> to divorce me when I got rid of the peanut butter
> that was full of additives and replaced it with a
> natural brand. Now, several months after the fact,
> everyone has calmed down, our house is running
> smoothly, and we do not use sugar or white flour.
> We use very little caffeine or salt. It has been a very
> difficult period for all of us. I love chocolate cake,
> cream pies, eclairs, you name it. I really believed I
> was showing love for my children when I brought
> them pumpkin cookies at Halloween and turkey
> shaped cookies at Thanksgiving . . . any excuse I
> could find. I trained my children to crave sugar.
>
> Then one day it was gone. Frosted Flakes down
> the drain. No more cakes. It just stopped. However,
> my advice to others would be to take it one step at a
> time. First the sugar cereals, then over a period of
> time the cookies, then the ice cream, then replace
> the white bread with wheat bread, and so on.
>
> We can't go back. I won't. My children have be-
> come aware of how food affects them, physically and
> emotionally. They have become label readers, which
> makes me happy. This will stand them in good stead
> all of their lives.
>
> —Gail Cutler, mom

Exercise

THE RALPH NADER GAME

What you're going to look for in this detective game is ways in which the food industry tries to manipulate you into buying foods that are not necessarily good for you.

Set up the search as a competition. The family member who finds the most "hidden persuaders" in a week becomes that week's Ralph Nader. If the children are small and would enjoy it, you might even have a badge such as an apple pin or some other representation of a healthy item of food that passes from week to week into the possession of the winner.

To arm your children properly for playing the game, you will have to teach them the basic food-industry ploys that they need to look for. They will learn these eagerly, however, if you do not make the game into a punishing activity but instead help them to see that it is fun for everyone to do together.

Reading Labels: Explain to your children that ingredients are listed on food labels in descending order of quantity. This means that if sugar is first on the list of ingredients, that product contains more sugar than anything else. Teach them the other names for sugar and give one "Ralph Nader" point to each person who identifies a heavily sugared product from which all of you should stay away.

Understanding How the Store Is Organized: Show your children how the grocery store is organized:

snack foods and candy near the checkout counter for impulse buying, simple, unprocessed foods like fruits and vegetables at the ends of the store, where customers spend less time; and processed foods in the center parts of the store where customers spend more time. Show them how the highly sugared, salted, and advertised products are placed at children's eye level, so that they can be convinced to urge their parents to buy them.

Observing Packaging: Make your children aware of the role that packaging plays in the presentation and sale of food. Show them the bright colors and popular cartoon figures on sugared cereal boxes and the packages of other unhealthy, highly priced food items, and help them understand that those products are presented that way to entice children into wanting them because of their packaging.

Resisting TV Commercials: Teach your children to have a healthy skepticism about what they see on TV. This will not turn them into cynics. Indeed, it will improve their critical judgment, a highly important skill for them to carry through life. Break into their concentration when they are watching snack-food commercials on TV. Ask them about the believability of what they are seeing. Soon you will find yourself awarding "Ralph Nader" points for discrepancies they will be able to point out between what they see on TV and the realities of good nutrition.

14

The Only System That Works

Warmth and affection are the major ingredients in parent-child relationships that keep adolescents away from drug and alcohol abuse. . . .
—*Conclusion, Mount Sinai School of Medicine Study Sponsored by National Institute on Drug Abuse*

The changes in child-rearing practices in our country over the past three decades have produced children [who] are angry and depressed and have limited resources to cope with stress. . . . They want relief from stressful feelings. . . . There is a marked decrease in the tolerance to cope with stress. . . .
—*Dr. Armand M. Nicholi, Jr., Massachusetts General Hospital, Harvard University Medical School, teenage-drug-use researcher*

I can't emphasize enough the importance of a close parent-child relationship. I know that establishing and maintaining such a relationship isn't easy; that doesn't make it less important. If such a relationship exists, problems can be talked out.

209

From a kid's point of view, when someone you respect and who has mutual respect for you gives you advice, you think about it seriously. Authoritarian commands and threats, although they may be based on good intentions, often elicit opposite responses.
—*Michael Jackson, age 21, former drug user, author,* Doing Drugs

If parents do not love their children, a growth starts in [the child's] stomach. Eventually this feeling of not being loved will come out, even though it may be twenty years later. The results are disastrous.
—*Allen F. Rosin, divorce court judge, Chicago*

Our kids live in a tough, tough world.

Remember how simple Halloween used to be? Dressing up and giggling and having fun making up dangers to fear? Now there are routine reports of poisoned candies and razor-laced apples to worry about, and children are warned extensively about the real dangers they face out on the streets. Quite a different picture.

Remember when all of tomorrow stretched ahead, full of hope, when children were shielded from danger, and violence was a dimly perceived presence in the neighborhood and on TV? Now, there are nightly wars, bombings, and body counts in a constant parade before their eyes. They watch, terrified and confused, as the vivid specter of destruction threatens their future.

There is much to cause children anxiety.

Vance Packard, in *Our Endangered Children*, writes of "the cold, hard world outside the home." He observes that "the whole tilt of our society, our institutions and, yes, our family functioning is toward blighting our youngsters and burdening them with pain, anxiety and discouraging problems."

"We can't walk the streets anymore," a twelve-year-old girl testified before the House of Representatives Select

Committee on Youth, Children and Family not long ago. "Does our world have to be like this?" she asked the politicians. "Can't you please change it?"

There isn't much, in answer to her plea, that we can do as individuals to change the world our children live in. But there is one totally reliable antidote to it.

It is parents' love.

In my work with parents and children, I have never met anyone, adult or child, who couldn't respond to love. I have met plenty, adult and child, whom it was not easy to love.

Erma Bombeck, that wise humorist, when asked what she had learned from raising her children, replied, "That a child needs your love the most when he deserves it the least."

The value of love in raising children is a hard lesson for many parents to learn. When struggling with the mysteries and challenges of raising their kids, they often look right past the obvious answer, searching for something complex, something magical. There is nothing more magical than love.

I have met many parents who, having not been loved themselves as children, find loving awkward and difficult. Sometimes, as much as they want to love their children, they don't even know how to *begin*. The sad fact this demonstrates is how very deprived they were themselves.

We are all capable of change and growth. Because someone failed to teach you how to love when you were young, when the lesson could have been easy to learn, does not mean that you cannot learn. It is *never* too late to learn to love.

And I cannot emphasize enough the importance of love.

Anthropologist Ashley Montagu says,

> The most critical of all human needs and abilities is the need and the ability to love. It is the central,

the cardinal, of all the needs of humankind. In the
world in which we live, a world in which so many
have been unloved to death, a world in which there
is a frightful absence of love behind the show of love,
it is today more than ever necessary to understand
that it is only through love that we can achieve fulfill-
ment as healthy human beings.

Dr. Montagu defines love as

> . . . the communication to others, by demon-
> strative acts, of one's profound involvement in their
> welfare . . . the reassurance that . . . one will be
> standing by, giving them all the supports, stimula-
> tion, encouragement and succor they require for
> their growth and development as humane, fulfilled
> human beings; that they can depend on us, that we
> will never commit the supreme treason of letting
> them down when they stand in need of us, that we
> are with them all the way . . .

What can we do, Dr. Montagu asks, "if one is not as
fully loving as we have it in us to be?" The answer, he
says, "is simply to behave *as if* you were a loving person.
If you work at it long enough, someday you will wake up
and find that you have become what you have been doing,
for what you are is not what you think or believe or say,
but what you do."

The material that is covered in this book is the curriculum of my stress-education classes, and what makes
those classes work, what gives them a spectacular record
of success, is the love that goes into them. It is the best
kind of love—nonjudgmental, noncritical, supportive
love. The kind of love that parents give. It says to a child,
"I like touching you"; "I like holding you"; "I like listening to you."

It is this kind of love that makes children feel good about themselves. As I have said so often, and as I will continue to say wherever and whenever anyone will listen, children who feel good about themselves can handle anything that comes along in life.

Love is the key, the bottom line. Love means being there for your child, no matter what. It costs so little to give, and there is so much to be gained.

All the suggestions and exercises in this book are for the purpose of taking children seriously, of showing them that you love them. They are for giving your children the attention, the skills, and the attitudes that will help them feel better about themselves, so that they can become healthier kids, kids who grow into capable adults who know how to conquer stress.

I know that you can be this kind of parent. I believe in you. You have the strength, the capacity for growth, and the love.

I hope that this book can be an important part of what you and your child are building together.

BIBLIOGRAPHY

FOR PARENTS AND PROFESSIONALS

Adler, Alfred. *The Problem Child: The Life Style of the Difficult Child As Analyzed in Specific Cases.* New York: Capricorn Books, 1963.

Ames, Louise B., and Joan A. Chase. *Don't Push Your Pre-Schooler,* rev. ed. New York: Harper & Row, 1981.

Arden, Donald B. *High Level Wellness.* New York: Bantam, 1979.

Canfield, Jack, and H. Wells. *100 Ways to Enhance Self-Concept in the Classroom.* Englewood Cliffs, N.J.: Prentice-Hall, 1976.

Cherry, Clare. *Think of Something Quiet: A Guide for Achieving Serenity in Early Childhood Classrooms.* Belmont, Calif: Pitman Learning, 1981.

Chester, Jane. *Psychopathology of Childhood.* Englewood Cliffs, N.J.: Prentice-Hall, 1966.

Dreikurs, Rudolf, and Vicki Soltz. *Children the Challenge.* New York: Hawthorn/Dutton, 1964.

————, and Bernie Grunwald. *Maintaining Sanity in the Classroom,* 2nd ed. New York: Harper & Row, 1982.

Eimers, Robert, and Robert Aitchison. *Effective Parents, Responsible Children.* New York: 1977.

Elkind, David. *The Hurried Child: Growing Up Too Fast Too Soon.* Reading, Mass.: Addison-Wesley, 1981.

Faber, Adele, and Elaine Mazlish. *How to Talk So Kids Will Listen.* New York: Avon, 1980.

Feingold, M.D., Ben. *Why Your Child Is Hyperactive.* New York: Random House, 1975.

Fraiberg, Selma. *The Magic Years: Understanding and Handling the Problems of Early Childhood.* New York: Charles Scribner's Sons, 1959.

215

Gardner, Richard. *Understanding Children.* Creskill, N.J.: Creative Therapeutics, 1979.

Garmezy, Norman, and Michael Rutter. *Stress, Coping and Development in Children.* New York: McGraw-Hill, 1983.

Gay, Kathryn. *Body Talk.* New York: Charles Scribner's Sons, 1974.

Gordon, Sol. *The Teenage Survival Book.* New York: Times Books, 1981.

Harmin, Merril, and Saville Sax. *A Peaceable Classroom (Activities to Calm and Free Student Energies).* Minneapolis, Minn.: Winston Press, 1980.

Hyde, Margaret. *Know Your Feelings.* New York: Franklin Watts, 1975.

Kraft, A. *Are You Listening to Your Child?* New York: Walker, 1973.

LeShan, Eda. *What Makes Me Feel This Way? (Growing Up with Human Emotions).* New York: Collier Books, 1972.

Lupin, Mimi. *Peace, Harmony, Awareness: A Relaxation Program for Children.* Houston: Self Management Tapes.

McGough, Elizabeth. *Your Silent Language.* New York: William Morrow, 1974.

Medeiros, Donald C., Barbara J. Porter, and I. David Welch. *Children Under Stress (How to Help with the Everyday Stresses of Childhood).* Englewood Cliffs, N.J.: Prentice-Hall, 1983.

Miller, Lani, and Diane Rodgers. *We Love Your Body.* Washington, D.C.: Morse Press, 1979.

Miller, Mary Susan. *Child-Stress.* New York: Doubleday, 1982.

Montagu, Ashley. *Touching (The Human Significance of the Skin).* New York: Harper & Row, 1978.

Myers, Irma. *Why You Feel Down and What You Can Do About It.* New York: Charles Scribner's Sons, 1982.

Patton, R. G., and L. I. Gardner. *Growth Failure in Maternal Deprivation.* Springfield, Ill.: Charles C Thomas, 1963.

Samuels, M., and H. Bennett. *The Well Body Book.* New York: Random House, 1973.

Segal, Jeanne. *Feeling Great.* New York: Newcastle Publisher, 1983.

Selye, Hans. *Stress Without Distress.* Philadelphia and New York: Lippincott, 1974.

Silverman, A. F., M. E. Pressman, and H. W. Bartel. "Self-Esteem and Tactile Communication." *Journal of Humanistic Psychology* 13 (1973): 73–77.

Simonton, O. Carl, Stephanie Matthews-Simonton, and James Creighton. *Getting Well Again.* Los Angeles: J. P. Tarcher, 1978.

ON NUTRITION

Cheraskin, Emanuel. *Psycho-Dietetics.* New York: Bantam, 1976.

Duffy, William. *Sugar Blues.* Radnor, Penn.: Chilton Book Corp., 1975.

Fredericks, Carlton. *Eat Well, Get Well, Stay Well.* New York: Grosset & Dunlap, 1980.

———. *Nutrition Handbook—Your Key to Good Health.* Los Angeles, Calif.: Major, 1976.

Lansky, Vicki. *The Taming of the C.A.N.D.Y. Monster.* New York: Bantam, 1978.

Lasky, Michael. *The Complete Junk Food Book.* New York: McGraw-Hill, 1977.

Schauss, Alexander. *Diet, Crime and Delinquency.* Berkeley, Calif.: Parker House, 1981.

Scheinkin, David, Michael Schalter, and Richard Hutton. *Food, Mind and Mood.* New York: Warner, 1979.

Stevens, Laura, and Rosemary Stoner. *How to Improve Your Child's Behavior Through Diet.* New York: Doubleday, 1979.

KIDS' COOKBOOKS

Barkie, Karen. *Sweet and Sugarfree.* New York: St. Martin's Press, 1982.

Mago, Patricia. *The Sugarless Baking Book.* Brookline, Mass.: Autumn Press, 1979.

Pinkwater, Jill. *The Natural Snack Cookbook.* New York: Four Winds Press, 1975.

Williams, Jacqueline, and Goldie Silverman. *No Salt No Sugar No Fat Cookbook.* Concord, Calif.: Nitty-Gritty Cookbook, 1982.

FOR CHILDREN SEVEN TO TEN

Allison, Leonard. *An Inch of Candle.* New York: Fontana, 1080.

Blume, Judy. *Are You There, God? It's Me, Margaret.* New York: Dell Yearling, 1970. (Concerns of adolescence.)

———. *Tales of a Fourth Grade Nothing.* New York: Dell Yearling, 1972.

Brown, Margaret Wise, and Clement Burd. *The Goodnight Moon.* New York: Harper & Row, 1947.

Elkins, Dov Peretz. *Glad to Be Me.* Englewood Cliffs, N.J.: Prentice-Hall, 1976.

Fitzhugh, Louise. *Harriet the Spy.* New York: Dell Yearling, 1977. (Fitting in, growing up, identity issues.)

Greene, Constance. *A Girl Called Al.* New York: Dell Yearling, 1980. (Relationships, identity issues, sex roles.)

———. *I and Sproggy.* New York: Dell Yearling, 1978. (Relationships, friendship.)

Kastner, Eric. *Lottie and Lisa.* New York: Puffin, 1978. (Divorce.)

Landis, James. *Sisters Impossible.* New York: Bantam Skylark, 1979.

Mann, Peggy. *There Are Two Kinds of Terrible.* New York: Bantam, 1977. (Death, growing up.)

McLean, Susan. *Pennies for the Piper.* New York: Ace Tempo, 1981. (Death, loneliness.)

Neville, Emily. *It's Like This, Cat.* New York: Harper Trophy, 1963. (Self-sufficiency.)

Palmer, Patricia. *Liking Myself.* San Luis Obispo, Calif.: Impact Pubs., 1977.

———. *The Mouse, The Monster and Me.* San Luis Obispo, Calif.: Impact Pubs., 1977.

Paterson, Katherine. *Bridge to Terebithia.* New York: Avon, 1980. (Self-esteem, confusion of early adolescence.)

———. *The Great Gilly Hopkins.* New York: Avon, 1978.

Richards, Arlene, and David McKay. *How to Get It Together When Your Parents Are Coming Apart.* New York: Bantam, 1977.

Stiller, Richard. *Your Body Is Trying to Tell You Something.* New York: Harcourt Brace Jovanovich, 1979.

Utley, Allison. *A Traveller in Time.* New York: Puffin, 1978. (Identity issues, growing up.)

Viorst, Judith. *Alexander and the Terrible Horrible No Good Very Bad Day.* New York: Atheneum, 1977.

———. *My Mama Says There Aren't Any Zombies, Ghosts, Vampires, Creatures, Demons, Monsters, Fiends, Goblins or Things.* New York: Atheneum, 1977.

———. *The Tenth Good Thing About Barney.* New York: Atheneum, 1976. (Death of a cat.)

Walsh, Jill Patton. *Goldengrove.* New York: Puffin, 1972.

Williams, Margery. *Velveteen Rabbit.* New York: Avon, 1975.

Zerafa, Judy. *Go for It.* New York: Workman Publishing, 1982.

FOR CHILDREN TEN TO FOURTEEN

Arrick, Fran. *Chernowittz!* New York: Signet, 1983. (Racial prejudice.)

Blume, Judy. *Tiger Eyes.* New York: Dell, 1983. (Death, growing up.)

Childress, Alice. *A Hero Ain't Nothin but a Sandwich.* New York: Avon, 1973. (Growing up, identity formation.)

Cooper, Susan. *Dawn of Fear.* New York: Puffin, 1981. (Death.)

Cormier, Robert. *I Am the Cheese.* New York: Dell, 1980. (Growing up, identity.)

———. *The Bumblebee Flies Anyway.* New York: Delacorte, 1980. (Mental illness, death, belonging.)

———. *The Chocolate War.* New York: Dell, 1980. (Group pressure.)

Cunningham, Julia. *Come to the Edge.* New York: Avon, 1977.

———. *Flight of the Sparrow.* New York: Avon, 1981.

Knowles, John. *A Separate Peace.* New York: Bantam, 1960. (Death, relationships, adolescence.)

L'Engle, Madelaine. *And Both Were Young.* New York: Dell, 1983. (Relationships.)

———. *Meet the Austins.* New York: Dell, 1978. (Adolescent identity issues, belonging.)

———. *A Ring of Endless Light.* New York: Dell, 1979. (Adolescent identity issues, belonging.)

Lipsyte, Robert. *One Fat Summer*. New York: Signet, 1977.
(Alienation, prejudice.)
O'Neal, Zibby. *A Formal Feeling*. New York: Fawcett Books,
1982. (Divorce.)
————. *The Language of Goldfish*. New York: Viking, 1980.
(Growing up, mental illness.)
Pfeffer, Susan Beth. *About David*. New York: Dell, 1980.
(Death, suicide, adolescence.)

INDEX

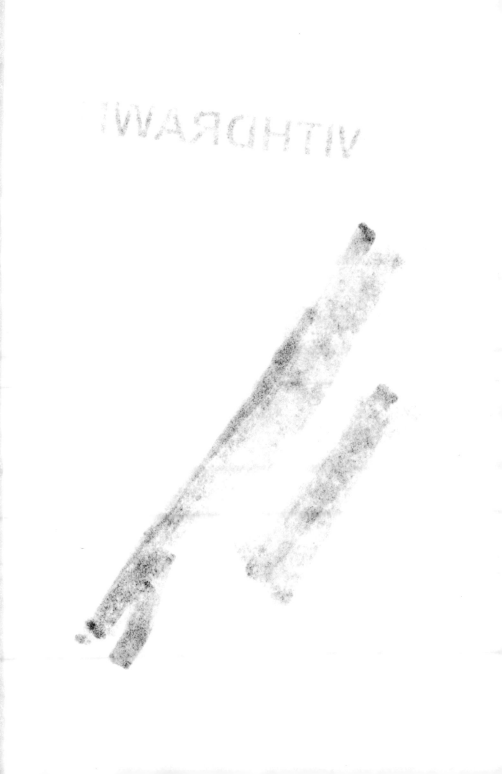

WITHDRAWN